WOMEN ROMANTIC POETS
ANNA BARBAULD AND
MARY ROBINSON

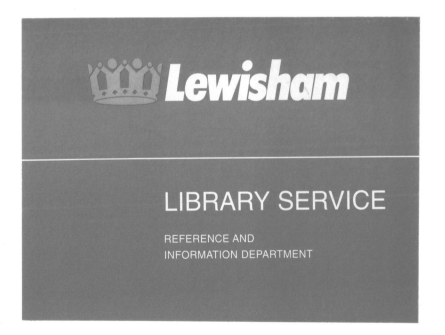

Lewisham

LIBRARY SERVICE

REFERENCE AND
INFORMATION DEPARTMENT

ANNA BARBAULD

MARY ROBINSON

From the original portrait by Sir Joshua Reynolds

WOMEN
ROMANTIC
POETS

ANNA BARBAULD
AND
MARY ROBINSON

Anne Janowitz

Northcote House
in association with the
British Council

© Copyright 2004 by Anne Janowitz

First published in 2004 by Northcote House Publishers Ltd, Horndon, Tavistock, Devon, PL19 9NQ, United Kingdom.
Tel: +44 (01822) 810066. Fax: +44 (01822) 810034.

British Library Cataloguing-in-Publication Data
A catalogue record for this book is available from the British Library

ISBN 0-7463-1029-3 hardcover
ISBN 0-7463-0896-5 paperback

Typeset by TW Typesetting, Plymouth, Devon
Printed and bound in the United Kingdom by
Athenaeum Press Ltd., Gateshead, Tyne & Wear

In Memory of Adeline Tintner

1912–2003

Scholar and Bibliophile

Contents

Acknowledgements

Grateful thanks to Drs Elizabeth Eger and Markman Ellis, and to Professor Isobel Armstrong, for reading this book in manuscript and offering helpful suggestions. Thanks as well to Robin Price for allowing me to read his fascinating paper on Anna Barbauld, which he was inspired to write when he lived in her house in Hampstead. I am grateful to Hilary Walford for her careful and persuasive corrections to the text.

Biographical Outlines

1743   Anna Aikin born, Kibworth Harcourt, Leicester-
        shire to Reverend John Aikin and Jane Jennings
        Aikin.
1758   Mary Darby born, Bristol, to Nicholas and Hen-
        rietta Darby.
        Aikin family moves to Warrington.
1773   Anna Aikin. *Poems*.
        Mary Darby marries Thomas Robinson, settles in
        London.
1774   Anna Aikin marries Rochemont Barbauld. Moves
        to Palgrave, Suffolk.
        Mary Robinson's daughter born, Maria Elizabeth
        Robinson.
1775   War with American Colonies begins.
        Thomas Robinson and family in Fleet Prison.
        Mary Robinson, *Poems*.
1777   Mary Robinson, *Captivity, A Poem; and Celadon, A
        Tale*.
1778   Anna Barbauld, *Lessons for Children from Two to
        Three Years Old*, *Lessons for Children of Three Years
        Old*.
1779   Mary Robinson performs as Perdita at Drury Lane
        Theatre. Begins love affair with Prince of Wales.
        Anna Barbauld, *Lessons for Children from Three to
        Four Years Old*.
1781   Anna Barbauld, *Hymns in Prose for Children*.
        Mary Robinson, in France, meets Marie Antoinette.
1782   Mary Robinson meets Banastre Tarleton.

1783	End of American War of Independence.
	Mary Robinson suffers disability en route to France.
1786–1787	Barbaulds move to London, then Hampstead.
1789	French Revolution begins with storming of the Bastille.
1790	Mary Robinson, *Ainsi va le monde*.
	Anna Barbauld, *Epistle to William Wilberforce, Esq. on the Rejection of the Bill for Abolishing the Slave Trade*.
	Anna Barbauld contributes to Toleration and Revolution Debate: *Address to the Opposers of the Repeal of the Corporation and Test Acts*.
1791	Mary Robinson, *Poems*.
1792	Anna Barbauld, *Civic Sermons to the People*.
	Anna Barbauld, *Remarks on Mr Gilbert Wakefield's Enquiry into the Expediency and Propriety of Public or Social Worship*.
1793	Anna Barbauld, *Sins of Government, Sins of the Nation*.
	Mary Robinson, *Poems* (2 vols.).
	Executions of Louis XVI and Marie-Antoinette.
	War between England and France begins.
1794	Treason Trials in Britain.
	Anna Barbauld recites Bürger's *Lenore* in Scotland.
1796	Mary Robinson, *Sappho and Phaon*.
1797	Anna Barbauld meets Coleridge.
1798	Mary Robinson writes *Memoirs*.
	Banastre Tarleton marries Susan Priscilla Bertie.
1799	Mary Robinson, *Letter to the Women of England, on the Injustice of Mental Subordination*.
	Mary Robinson, *The False Friend: A Domestic Story*.
	Mary Robinson, *The Natural Daughter: A Novel*.
	Mary Robinson, chief poetry contributor and editor for *Morning Post*.
1800	Mary Robinson meets Coleridge.
	Mary Robinson, *Lyrical Tales*. Dies 26 December.
	Mary Robinson and Anna Barbauld both included in Ogilvie's *Odes*.

1802	Barbaulds move to Stoke Newington.
1804	Anna Barbauld edits Richardson's *Correspondence*.
1807	Abolition of the Slave Trade.
1808	Rochemont Barbauld commits suicide, 11 November.
1810	Anna Barbauld edits and writes prefaces for *The British Novelists*.
1812	Anna Barbauld, *Eighteen Hundred and Eleven*.
1815	War between England and France ends.
1825	Anna Barbauld dies, 9 March.

Abbreviations and References

BARBAULD

PALB   *The Poems of Anna Laetitia Barbauld*, ed. William McCarthy and Elizabeth Kraft (London: University of Georgia Press, 1994)

RGW   *Remarks on Mr Gilbert Wakefield's Enquiry into the Expediency and Propriety of Public or Social Workship* (London: Johnson, 1792)

SPP   *Selected Poetry and Prose of Anna Laetitia Barbauld*, ed. William McCarthy and Elizabeth Kraft (Ontario: Broadview Press, 2002)

ROBINSON

C.   *Captivity, A Poem; and Celadon, A Tale* (London: T. Beckett, 1777)

LWE   *Letter to the Women of England, on the Injustice of Mental Subordination* (London: Longman, 1799)

Per.   *Perdita: The Memoirs of Mary Robinson*, ed. M. J. Levy (London: Peter Owen, 1994)

P.   *Poems* (London: C. Parker, 1775)

PWMR   *Poetical Works of the Late Mrs. Mary Robinson*, 3 vols. (London: R. Phillips, 1806)

SP   *Selected Poems*, ed. Judith Pascoe (Ontario: Broadview Press, 2000)

1

Sense and Sensibility

The aim of this book is to introduce readers to the lives and works of Anna Laetitia Barbauld and Mary Robinson, two of the most influential women poets of the late eighteenth and early nineteenth centuries. Along with Wordsworth and Coleridge and Southey, they defined the themes of Romantic poetry, exploring the interiority of the self and the relation of self to society and nature; and they made immense claims for the power of poetry as a way of both knowing and changing the world. Anna Barbauld's poetry of social intimacy was the original 'conversation' poem, later practised by Coleridge. As poetry editor of the *Morning Post* in the late 1790s, Mary Robinson published both her own and William Wordsworth's experiments in making the ballad a form for representing the subjectivity of the outcast.

Though Barbauld and Robinson can both be described as Romantic poets, their places with respect to one another within this capacious category are anything but congruent. I have imaged the antithetical complementarity of Mrs Barbauld and Mrs Robinson as *Sense and Sensibility*, a contrast readers will recognize as belonging to Jane Austen's novel. I, too, aim for some irony in making so stark a division. As 'Sense', Mrs Barbauld works up the poetic language of Enlightenment rationalism from within the religious perspective of deism, reflecting her own education through the polite restraint of Dissenting sociability. As 'Sensibility', Mrs Robinson makes emotional poetry out of what Coleridge called her 'full and overflowing' mind, drawn from the drama of the demi-monde of actresses and courtesans, and surrounded by the excessive appetites of the Prince of Wales's Whig acolytes. Mrs Barbauld is seemly; Mrs Robinson bursts at the seams. But these vivid contrasts are overly schematic. Mrs Barbauld's sense is infiltrated by a set of passionate responses to intellectual and political issues, and her writing and theories articulated through what can be described as 'devotional sensibility', while her life history forced her to confront the extremes of emotional violence. Mrs Robinson, for all the overt sentiment of her poems and many novels, was acutely practical. Barbauld's Enlightenment roots drew her into political radicalism; Robinson was, on the other hand, a *cultural* radical, making her poetry out of her personal experience of trying to forge a life for herself through work – without financial or matrimonial protection. Mrs Barbauld conveyed a precarious poetic austerity in the face of her husband's murderous rages, Mary Robinson maintained the rigorous discipline of daily work – acting, writing, and editing – in the midst of public and disastrous love affairs, financial crisis, and serious physical disability.

Barbauld and Robinson both occupied the same city (London) at roughly the same time (the last decades of the eighteenth century), and, despite differences of education, wealth, and religion, lived in overlapping social circles and shared some important political and poetic values and ambitions. Although a comparative case study of these two poets does not exhaustively account for 'women Romantic poets', to try and cover more than two poets in a study of this length would lead either to false generalizations about women's poetry in the period or to a recalcitrant jumble of names, dates, and details.

This study explores how these particular women gained access to their vocations as public intellectuals and poets. One of the things that commanded my attention, and at times admiration, when writing this study is how they struggled to become *themselves*. How did Anna Laetitia Aikin, the cherished clever daughter of a provincial Dissenter, become, in the context of the London intelligentsia of the 1780s and 1790s, Anna Barbauld the radical polemicist? Her public writing blossomed within the overlapping discussions of Dissenting enfranchisement and French Revolution republicanism, after years at home in the distinguished Dissenting Academy at

Warrington, and as a 'good wife' and educationalist in Suffolk. In the case of Mary Robinson, what does it mean that she was able to drift from being a *demi-mondaine* in the arch and spectacular world of aristocratic Whig politico-sex (not to be entirely distinguished from sexual politics) to being a late-1790s prototype of what would become nineteenth-century middle-class sentimental Romanticism?

Literary historians and critics have discovered a wealth of materials about and articulated the links between the late-eighteenth-century poetic of sensibility and the Romantic poetic that dominated English poetry from the early nineteenth century onwards. Contemporary critics such as Judith Pascoe, Anne Mellor, Isobel Armstrong, Elizabeth Eger, Jerome McGann, Markman Ellis, G. J. Barker-Benfield, Moira Ferguson, William McCarthy, Elizabeth Ty, and Stuart Curran have explored the ways sensibility – what Addison called 'a kind of quick and delicate feeling in the soul' – allowed and encouraged women to explore experience in a language proceeding from the heart. One group of these critics has found a set of coded struggles against patriarchal authority within much of the poetics of sensibility. This approach asserts that women writers found ways of presenting their critical positions in the available poetic conventions of sympathy, virtue, and responsiveness. Isobel Armstrong's very important essay 'The Gush of the Feminine' starts from this premiss, but critically augments the argument by articulating a theory of emotional intellectualism, the dialectical ties of reason and feeling.[1] Another critical pathway, related but distinct, has found examples in the poetry of sensibility of how women's poetic interests were suppressed and maimed by patriarchy: William McCarthy and Eleanor Ty have both made impressive arguments of this kind.[2] Through the recent expansion of the poetic archive, poems by Coleridge and Wordsworth, Byron, Keats, Shelley, now share space and importance with poems by Charlotte Smith, Anna Barbauld, and Mary Robinson amongst the first generation of Romantic poets, and poems by Letitia Landon and Felicia Hemans amongst the second generation.

Anna Barbauld and Mary Robinson, variously considered distinguished, famous, infamous, and outrageous in their own period, have been beneficiaries of 1980s and 1990s feminist

3

criticism. William Hazlitt, often considered the most progressive Romantic essayist, who might be expected to have cham-
pioned Barbauld's rationalism, arrogantly patronized her as a
'pretty poetess'.[3] And, though Hazlitt defended Mary Robinson against William Gifford's 1794 satire the *Baviad*, which
coruscated the Della Cruscan poets, with whom Robinson was
associated for a time, by the end of the nineteenth century the
Dictionary of National Biography described her poetry as 'jejune,
affected, and inept', and her talents 'imaginary'.

The increased use of primary historical materials within the
study of poetics has extended the range of questions we can
ask about women Romantic poets, and with greater access to
what were earlier considered ephemeral materials – periodicals, newspapers, and pamphlet literature – we have more
detailed information about how these women thought about
their worlds and how they presented themselves. We now look
with greater interest to those issues that vitally concerned the
writers under scrutiny – questions of religion, of social ties, of
formal education, of poetic calling and ambition, and of the
political and cultural consequences of their work as writers.

This discussion places two women poets in a context of
comparison. By using them to think about each other, we may
be able to learn things about how they understood themselves
and their poetic vocations within their own time. I will not
spend much time on how Barbauld and Robinson have been
interpreted since the 1980s, but focus instead on how they
made sense to themselves and to others in their lifetimes.

ANNA LAETITIA BARBAULD, NÉE AIKIN

Readers of Romantic poetry frequently first meet Anna Laetitia
Aikin Barbauld through her peculiarly visionary and empirical
survey of the contemporary world, *Eighteen Hundred and
Eleven*. We often start with this poem, and then stay with it
(certainly scholars do: the greatest number of critical articles on
Barbauld's poetry discuss *Eighteen Hundred and Eleven*), because its voice is so confident, its poetic and political reach
global, its vision of futurity dreadful to Britain but exciting to
the world:

4

> Britain, know,
> Thou who hast shared the guilt [of 'Luxury' and 'Want'] must
>   share the woe . . .
> The golden tide of Commerce leaves thy shore . . .
> Leaves thee, perhaps, to visit distant lands,
> And deal the gifts of Heaven with equal hands.
>
> (*SPP* 163, ll. 45–6, 62, 65–6)

Eighteen Hundred and Eleven is not a generically unusual poem; it takes up the common eighteenth-century poetic theme of the westward movement of the course of empire, a theme that emphasizes both the prosperity of the imperial city and its future evanescence.[4] In 1740, in *The Ruins of Rome*, John Dyer wrote a Whig version of the problem of the decline of empire. Comparing England to Rome as mercantile and trading centres, Dyer suggested that England was analogous to Rome, and therefore threatened by the same abyss of decline. But Dyer's moralization of the scene of ruin ends by affirming English self-consciousness, and asserts the nation's ability to withstand the depredations of both time and corruption. In the westward course of things, England was now the centre of the world: brought into being through political, commercial, intellectual, and artistic achievements. Seventy-one years later Anna Barbauld's version of the ruin poem was received as an insult by the literary establishment, even by those who would think of themselves as free from conformism in either politics or aesthetics. As the nineteenth century finished its first decade, and approached the end of its second decade of war with France, while Barbauld moved to the end of her sixth (she was 68 when she wrote the poem), she sounded a less than triumphant tone and she stated overtly her anxiety about decline. London, world city, which had held 'forth the book of life to distant lands', now finds 'The worm is in thy core, thy glories pass away; / Arts, arms and wealth destroy the fruits they bring' (*SPP* 173, ll. 314–15). Barbauld's poem moralizes a set of ruins that evoke not past splendours, but the burgeoning metropolis of the present. The dialectics of time and space, however, will again take the course of empire westward further, and with even better results: 'Thy world, Columbus, shall be free' (*SPP* 173, l. 334). Barbauld is able to imagine and even welcome the supercession of British Empire – something that makes her kin to other liberal writers such as Constantin-François Volney and Percy Bysshe Shelley. We cannot know precisely what gave her the ability to look beyond her own time and place. In part it must have been the psychological privilege of advancing age: she had written in 1804 that 'it is equally true of books as of their authors, that one generation passeth away and another cometh'. Linked to that optimistic fatalism was her political boldness, which produced out of the polemical point about domestic corruption a turn on the poetic convention: her poem on the course of empire does not stop in the present tense. Barbauld's long personal association with London life is also important for *Eighteen Hundred and Eleven*. She spent a considerable amount of time in London from the early 1780s and she lived in Hampstead and Stoke Newington until her death in 1825. She knew London as both the local community of neighbourhood and a thriving metropolis, and she was particularly alert to its living relationship to its inhabitants. For Barbauld as for Mary Robinson, crucial aspects of her intellectual identity were forged through metropolitan freedoms. The ambivalence that shapes *Eighteen Hundred and Eleven* turns on the meanings of those city freedoms – both dizzying the self and authorizing its power. In her poem the metropolis is a great estate of diversity and possibility, with 'No jealous drawbridge, and no closing gate' (*SPP* 167, l. 162). Although Barbauld did not write many poems about London, she seems most herself when commenting on its value *and* its ephemerality – 'Commerce, like beauty, knows no second spring' – and on its cruelty: 'With grandeur's growth the mass of misery grows' (*SPP* 173, ll. 316, 320). *Eighteen Hundred and Eleven* was the last public poem Barbauld was to publish, and it generated hot criticism in the press. To her critics, she was too old, too unpatriotic, too unlike herself as the pedagogue and poet of devotional sensibility. This poem would not do in a culture of insularity and instability. The harsh reception was a blow to Barbauld, and its shock an instance of her lifelong cultural naivety working in tandem with her equally lifelong commitment to social and political justice.

We finish *Eighteen Hundred and Eleven* with a sense of its strong persona, that idiosyncratic identity that was both the

6

price and the prize of Anna Barbauld's journey to London. Both Anna Barbauld and Mary Robinson started out in the provinces. In her autobiographical writing, Robinson narrates her own youth in Bristol as the *prehistory* to her creative life in London; but Barbauld appears to us as having been born with the characteristics that would serve her through life. Chief amongst these was her rational rigour. An anecdote recorded by the Dissenter Newcome Cappe recalls the 4-year-old Anna Aikin demonstrating her precocious intellect: her father was discussing a doctrinal issue with a pupil over a meal, and he made the point that

'Joy, accurately defined, cannot have place in a state of perfect felicity; for joy supposes an *accession* of happiness.' 'I think you are mistaken, Papa,' exclaimed a little voice from the opposite side of the table. 'Why do you think so, Laetitia?'

'Because Papa, in the chapter I read to you this morning in the Testament, it said there is more joy in heaven over one sinner that repented than over 99 just persons that need no repentance.'[5]

This early preciosity was nurtured in the provincial setting of the Dissenting Academy in Warrington, under the close direction of her father, Warrington's Divinity Tutor, John Aikin, DD, and strongly influenced by Joseph Priestley, a chief architect of Rational Dissent. Later, her identity as an educationalist grew in tandem with her work with her husband, Rochement Barbauld. At Palgrave they created a boarding school for boys. But it was in London that she forged her identity as an independent reforming intellectual and polemicist. Barbauld's physical journey from province to metropolis and her intellectual journey from the polite poetry of her years in Warrington to her London-forged passionate polemic was also a social journey from the society of the familiar and comfortable Warrington Dissenting circle to the miscellany of classes, occupations, and backgrounds that contributed to the physical and intellectual variety of London. While many people's development can be described on the model of sexual coming of age, Barbauld's ascent into personal autonomy can be mapped as a set of increasingly complex geographical locations.

MARY DARBY ROBINSON

The variety of London allowed Anna Barbauld, if only for a time, to slough off the thick wall of her secure self-identity and experience creative uncertainty. Mary Robinson, quite differently, found in the metropolis a series of plausible and self-created identities.[6] Tabitha Bramble, Oberon, Laura Maria, Sappho, Mary Robinson: the woman born as Mary Darby used all these names to sign some of the most widely read and valued English poetry written during the final years of the eighteenth century. Perdita, Jane Shore, Rosalind, and Cordelia: these are names of imagined women whose roles she took on as a London actress between 1776 and 1780. Actress, poet, novelist, political writer, editor: Mary Robinson had an enormously diverse and triumphant career, undertaking in twenty years labours that today would at the very least be considered stressful. At the same time, she was a devoted mother and both mistress and confidante of men and women at the centre of Whig politics and sociability in the volatile years leading up to and during the Regency. She was an active member of the 1780s and 1790s intelligentsia: that mixture of reform-minded aristocrats, liberal and even republican radicals, middle-class philanthropic and bluestocking women, writers, painters, and playwrights. She corresponded with William Godwin the philosopher, defended Mary Wollstonecraft the feminist, was friends with Southey and Coleridge, as well as with political insiders such as the Whig Charles James Fox, who at the time he knew Robinson served as Foreign Secretary in both the Rockingham and Coalition ministries, and as Secretary of the Treasury under Shelburne. Robinson's friends and patrons included the great actor and proprietor of the Drury Lane theatre, David Garrick, and the playwright Richard Brinsley Sheridan, as well as the powerful aristocrat, Georgiana, Duchess of Devonshire. Robinson travelled amongst the more glamorous London sets of actors and gamblers: she was a frequent visitor to London's pleasure gardens and parks, and, as mistress to the Prince Regent, she entertained and was entertained in the most sparkling rooms of West End society.[7]

While my interest in Robinson in this comparative study is her importance as a poet and as an influential shaper of poetic

8

taste, it is difficult to present and assess her work without some attention to her life as actress, political intellectual, and 'It' girl. Although attention to the private life of a writer may not always be helpful, knowing about Mary Robinson's life is important for understanding her work, because she lived the paradox of leading a very *public* life characterized by its display of apparently *private affections* and concerns. Literary historians of the Romantic period write of Byron as the first 'celebrity' of the modern age, but Mary Robinson had been one twenty years earlier. *Vancenza, or, the Dangers of Cruelty* (1792), Robinson's first novel, was sold out in a day and went through five editions in rapid succession, just as Byron's *Childe Harold* was to make him famous overnight. Serious literary interpretation of Robinson's work ran alongside public gossip about her private life. The pages of London newspapers such as the *Morning Herald* and the *Morning Post*, whose poetry page Mary Robinson was to dominate in the last years of her life, had earlier published squibs about her doings in society and on its edges. Her affair with the Prince Regent was exposed to the reading public the way the private lives of our present-day public figures are, though perhaps more coyly:

> A certain young actress who leads the *ton* appeared in the side-box at the Haymarket Theatre . . . with all the grace and splendour of a Duchess, to the no small mortification of the female world, and the astonishment of every Spectator. (*Morning Post*, 16 July 1780)

Robinson's cultural environs in the West End were very different from Barbauld's in St Paul's and Hampstead and Stoke Newington, even though, as we shall see, their poetic and political interests coincided and their paths crossed in the 1790s. Though her audience extended beyond her immediate circle, Mrs Barbauld was a poet who felt herself to be securely positioned at the heart of a homogeneous circle of close friends and family made even more compact by their status as Dissenters. For the most part, her back was turned to the public, who saw her as if in the reflection of a mirror. Mary Robinson, on the other hand, appears to us vividly and as if always amongst acquaintances rather than friends, frequently outdoors in the urban movement of carriages driving through the London parks, even though she spent much of her life in semi-seclusion, unable to walk after an injury and perhaps miscarriage at the age of 23. We see her in London public spaces, facing the public, and, willingly or not, presenting her private self in public performance and poetic text. Her final act of self-display was her *Memoirs*, begun by Robinson, and then posthumously completed and edited by her daughter. The *Memoirs* aimed to weave into a single life story the variety of personae she had built and then inhabited over her forty-one years.[8]

This book argues that Barbauld and Robinson were both important radical poets of their time: but that Barbauld's was fundamentally an Enlightenment rationalist radicalism, while Robinson's was essentially a type of cultural radicalism. Anna Barbauld was a poetic conservative and a political radical; Robinson was first of all a cultural radical, and that pulled in its wake a set of changing political attitudes. Barbauld was raised as and remained an advocate of the liberal implications of Enlightenment thought. Rationality, compassion, and democratic human rights were the mainstays of her political positions. Her work from start to finish presents this, and she also saw the ways in which religious experience might be linked to these principles. It is the unwavering consistency of Barbauld's Enlightenment political-poetics from the 1770s through to 1811 that made her values appear to be dated when she published *Eighteen Hundred and Eleven*.

Mary Robinson, on the other hand, was a cultural and social radical; she was the harbinger of the sentimental romanticism of individualism. Because of her own experience of social dislocation, Robinson was able, more than either Barbauld or Wordsworth, to summon her massive intelligence to understand those who shared, albeit in quite different ways, her sense of how disruption shapes emotional experience. This is part of what makes her an avant-gardist of life. Her poetry was always experimental in being an ongoing essay in self-improvement. In her best, also her last volume of poems, *Lyrical Tales* (1800), Robinson links the motive of romantic interiority to the social issues of poverty and displacement. Robinson is self-making and self-reliant, while Barbauld is more at ease with herself and also more compliant with respect to authority. In these responses to their environments, we catch the difference between coming of age in the height of the overt values of the British Enlightenment and in the culture of sensibility and inwardness, for Anna Barbauld was born in 1743, Mary Robinson in 1758.

Barbauld remains impressive for the ways in which she maintained her politics throughout her lifetime; Robinson astonishes by the ways in which she adapts and dialectically engages with the swiftly changing world around her. Barbauld is made by her world – an Emma Woodhouse figure; Robinson makes herself. Robinson adumbrates the later romantic heroine, Marguerite Gautier, the lady of the camellias – splendid, brilliant, passionate, and sentimental. I admire Anna Barbauld's politics, and am more in mental sympathy with her than with Robinson, but it is hard not to want to be the heroine of one's own romance – as was Mary Robinson.

2

Poetic Vocation and Polite Letters: The 1760s and 1770s

While, to nineteenth-century readers she was the elderly and somewhat forbidding 'Mrs Barbauld', Barbauld's first volume of *Poems* appeared under her maiden name of Aikin, and it was as Anna Aikin that her reputation as a poet was established in the 1770s. The volume, which appeared in 1773 under the imprint of the Dissenting London publisher, Joseph Johnson, was Aikin's entry into the world of polite letters, her first poems to reach an audience wider than the small circle of family and friends in Warrington amongst whom she lived from the age of 15 to 30, from adolescence to adulthood. Two years later a book similar in both size and content, *Poems by Mrs. Robinson*, was published by Parker of New Bond Street, and it too announced the author's entry into public letters. For both women, publication was a source of pride and anxiety: their work was now open to review and comment, and might bring them fame or shame.

Neither volume is poetically adventurous: both are conventional in relation to the fashions of sensibility. Both Aikin and Robinson include a mix of pastoral, meditative, and lyric poems, and both include a large number of poems that address or describe friends – typical addressees of poetry of sympathy – as distinct from the poetic tradition of romantic passions, directed to the 'Beloved'. But the two offer up differences as well as unremarkable similarities: Aikin's poetry carries a strong sense of both personal and poetic self-confidence, and is uttered in a clear and forceful voice. Mary Robinson's *Poems* of 1775 was the work of a 16 year old, who, though having had some education during a peripatetic childhood, learned early on how to please by adhering to whatever model of self-presentation she judged appropriate. Anna Aikin's volume is the work of a woman about to turn 30, whose poems had been circulating privately for some time in a milieu in which occasional poetry writing was considered a normal accomplishment. For Robinson, the test of her work was the degree to which it 'passed' as standard and polite; for Aikin, her task was to push beyond the limits of drawing-room accomplishments and find her own voice. Despite different ratios of talent to skill, and different proportions of nature and nurture, these first volumes are analogous. And because Anna Aikin confidently accepted the poetic forms of polite letters, this chapter begins with *her* access to poetic vocation. It is also the case that Aikin's work inspired Mary Robinson. In her *Memoirs* Robinson recalled the occasion when she first read Aikin's *Poems* with the enthusiasm of an acolyte and the envy of a competitor: 'I read them with rapture; I thought them the most beautiful Poems I had ever seen, and considered the woman who could invent such poetry, as the most to be envied of human creatures' (*Per.* 54–5). Within two years her own volume had been published.

ANNA BARBAULD AS ANNA AIKIN, DAUGHTER AND SISTER

Anna Laetitia Aikin was born in 1743 in the village of Kibworth in Leicestershire, and at the age of 15 she moved with her family to Warrington, near Liverpool, when her father was appointed as tutor at the just-founded Academy at Warrington. Anna Aikin was formed as a young poet in an intellectual atmosphere that today we would call 'progressive pedagogy'. The Dissenting Academy at Warrington was founded as one of a series of establishments to train Nonconformist clergy, who had been excluded from public life from the time of Charles II's Corporation and Test acts of 1661 and 1673, legislation that rendered Nonconformists second-class citizens until 1828. The strength of the Warrington institution was chiefly in science and letters: there was a strong secular strain to the curriculum, and it drew from a wide social base of sons of planters, professionals, and manufacturers, including families who belonged to the Established Church, but who felt their sons would get a better education in the intellectually advanced and apparently more disciplined Dissenting educational milieu.[1] Dissenting education influenced the social fields it wished to conquer. The English Enlightenment, as it absorbed and developed ideas from both Europe and Scotland, was strengthened in the Dissenting intelligentsia. Joseph Priestley, the scientist who first isolated the properties of oxygen and the reformer who campaigned for civil liberties, was an important influence on the Warrington Academy's curriculum while he served there as the Modern Languages tutor from 1761 until 1767. Priestley introduced lectures on politically useful subjects that ran in tandem with the religious teaching on which the Academy was founded; these included 'History and General Policy', 'Laws and Constitutions of England', and the 'History of England'. He later recalled: 'This I did in consequence of observing that, though most of our pupils were young men designed for situations in civil and active life, every article in the plan of their Education was adapted to the learned professions.'[2] Priestley advocated the kind of learning that would service the new citizen-managers of a growing industrial and governmental apparatus. If Dissenters were themselves kept out of office, men such as Priestley believed this would not long be the case. What appeared to be the clear and steady path towards integration, however, was interrupted during the period of the wars with France (1793–1815), as it appeared to many people that the causes of Dissent and those of revolutionary ardour were too closely linked. At the same time, as families outside the Dissenting community also sent their sons to Warrington for its emphasis on civil society, the connections grew ever stronger between political insiders and the Dissenting intellectual and scientific outsiders.

After the academy's closure in 1786, Warrington's reputation served as an emblem of what liberal pedagogy might rise to, 'distinguished by sound learning, just and liberal principles, and virtuous manners'.[3] The pedagogic goal was to produce what Anna Aikin made legible in her *Poems* of 1773 as 'a well-tuned mind' (*PALB* 69, l. 1). The Warrington tutors aimed to incarnate an ideal of social intercourse conceived of as

14

informal, familiar, and amiable, teaching the virtues of 'candid manners' and an 'active mind' (*PALB* 68, l. 11). The history of the Warrington Academy was mythologized and made widely available by a Warrington student, William Turner. In 1813, some twenty-five years after the Academy had closed, Turner's narrative was published in the *Monthly Repository*, the central periodical of the Unitarian intelligentsia.[4] The *Monthly Repository* was similar in orientation to Joseph Johnson's *Analytical Review* and as well to journals edited by Anna Aikin's brother, John Aikin, which included the *Monthly Magazine* and the *Athenaeum*, and to the *Annual Review*, edited by her nephew, Arthur Aikin. Closest to it, and named in part for its sake, was Priestley's *Theological Repository*, founded in 1769. The *Monthly Repository* would become the great Unitarian/Benthamite journal of the Victorian period, and the public archive of Unitarian dissent. Anna Barbauld published some poems and memoirs in the first series edited by Robert Aspland. In the 1770s, the Aikin family itself presented its own aims and those of the Academy as inextricably interconnected, encapsulated in Turner's phrase 'free familiar conversation'.[5] This renown depended upon personal as well as public reports of its polite sociability, told, for example, in the sermon William Enfield delivered at Anna's father's funeral. And it was he, John Aikin, DD, who was credited with introducing many of the informal norms of instructional life there. The nineteenth-century history of Warrington's reputation was augmented by Anna's niece Lucy's memoir of her own father (Anna Aikin's brother), John Aikin, MD, and it was further brought into the literary arena through memoirs of Anna Barbauld by both Lucy Aikin and her great-niece, Anna Le Breton.[6] The Aikin family continued its history of itself well into the twentieth century with Betsy Rodgers's family history, *Georgian Chronicle*.[7] Anna Aikin's 1773 *Poems* was a founding document in the public life of Warrington's private virtues. As we shall see, while Anna's volume was launched as part of a family and institutional project, Mary Robinson's was an isolated bid or offering to become part of some larger community.

The foundational Warrington sociable norms promoted by the network of clerical and civic men, which even the cranky and unreconstructed radical Gilbert Wakefield recalled in his

Memoirs as a 'feast of reason and of soul', were codified through the writings of their female descendants, itself a consequence of Warrington's self-conscious assimilation of the schoolroom to the parlour. Anna's reiteration of the value of the family and familial bonds, articulated in her poems and in her pedagogic writings, was restated by her niece Lucy Aikin as the domesticity of an extended family: 'I have often thought with envy of that society,' she wrote in a letter to the Lancashire historian Henry Bright; 'they [the tutors] and theirs lived together like one large family'.[8] This domesticity linked tutors, students, and families via an idealized notion of intellectual freedom: a familiarity in which, Aikin writes, 'pleasing fires of lively fancy play, / And wisdom mingles her serener ray' (*PALB* 2, ll. 47–8). Lucy Aikin's narrative of Warrington reported that: 'The most cordial intimacy subsisted among the tutors and their families, with whom also the elder students associated on terms of easy and affectionate inter-course.'[9] Barbauld's development as a poet is presented in both her own words and by those written about her, as emerging from within the Warrington ethos.

But the Warrington Academy was not a family: it was a pioneering provincial institution. It numbered some of the most significant educationalists among the Dissenting branches of Presbyterians and Congregationalists, and from it emerged important scientific, radical, and reform thinkers and publications. Warrington provided the intellectual counterpart to the commercial and technological growth sponsored by Quakers.[10] By the 1780s these Nonconformists felt themselves to be on the cusp of fully entering into English social and political life, anticipating the repeal of the Corporation and Test acts. Having developed the economic infrastructure for political power through its commercial and industrial interests as well as producing scientific and literary innovation outside the establishment, the Dissenting milieu could claim a pristine intellectual and moral authority – not holding public office meant Dissenters could not be accused of corruption, and the intellectual self-confidence inspired by such a position runs through the rhetoric of various Warringtonians. Warrington's political discourse was principled and enlightened, shaped by the Aikins and Gilbert Wakefield and Joseph Priestley, all

16

active campaigners in the 1780s on issues of religious reform, abolition of the slave trade, and scientific research. The first poem in Anna Aikin's *Poems*, 1773, 'Corsica', suggests that current political issues were part and parcel of everyday discussion and enthusiasms.

> The man devoted to the public, stands
> In the bright records of superior worth
> A step below the skies.
>
> (*SPP* 64, ll. 126–8)

Within the confines of being at home Anna Aikin imagines the ways in which political struggle ignites the mind:

> 'Tis not meats, and drinks,
> And balmy airs, and vernal suns, and showers
> That feed and ripen minds; 'tis toil and danger;
> And wrestling with the stubborn gripe of fate.
>
> (*SPP* 64–5, ll. 155–8)

So, interwoven with the polite manners of free familiarity were the more pressing and topical political issues that came from this combination of political exclusion and philosophical Enlightenment. Warrington students were a politically strong-minded lot: amongst young scholars were Malthus, many later MPs, and a large number of scientists and writers. At moments these ambitious and outspoken students even shocked their tutors, who were alarmed and terrified at the anti-English zeal, which, during the 'American war, was displayed by several of the students. One of them, who boarded at Dr Enfield's, insisted on his right to illuminate *his own* windows for an American victory; but this the Doctor declined to allow, as it committed himself, the master of the house.'[11]

ANNA AIKIN'S POETIC APPRENTICESHIP

This should suggest something of the intellectual and social world within which the young Anna Aikin led her charmed, if also circumscribed life. She was considered prodigious from the start. An affectionate letter from her mother recalls:

I once indeed knew a little girl who was as eager to learn as her instructors could be to teach her, and who, at two years old, could read sentences and little stories in her *wise book*, roundly, without spelling, and in a half a year more could read as well as most women; but I never knew such another, and I believe never shall.[12]

Having persuaded her father to allow her to learn Greek and Latin, Anna Aikin was a ready interlocutor for the Warrington students and tutors.[13] But, though Warrington served her well, it apparently did not suggest to her to that it might serve as a model institution for other young women, and it is somewhat disheartening to learn that she turned down the bluestocking Elizabeth Montagu's request to help start a 'kind of Academy' for young women. Aikin replied to Montagu that the 'best way for a woman to acquire knowledge is from conversation with a father or brother'. She asserted: 'my own situation has been peculiar, and would be no rule for others.'[14] In fact, in her circle her own education *was* undertaken through conversation with father and brother, but within an institutional setting that itself aimed in its ethos to blend together the familial and the educational. She might well have had an idealized notion that the boundaries of the domestic scene were very porous, and her early poems suggest her own awareness of her special place and her equanimity within that 'peculiar' extended family.

As William McCarthy has pointed out, over a third of Aikin's poems were written before she was 30, but it seems that hardly any were written before she was about 24 (*PALB*, p. xxix). Her poems then were those of an adult living within a parental regime. Writing poetry was an accomplishment of polite society practised by many Warrington tutors. Anna's younger brother John began writing early on, and had imagined a literary life for himself. Later in his own life, Joseph Priestley asserted both his own poetic talents and their influence on the more poetically celebrated Anna:

In the early part of my life, I was a great versifier . . . Mrs Barbauld has told me that it was the perusal of some verses of mine, that first induced her to write anything in verse, so that this country is in some measure indebted to me for one of the best poets it can boast of.[15]

POEMS, 1773

Taken as a group, the poems Barbauld wrote when she was Anna Aikin, a young woman at Warrington, formulate her notions of intellectual friendship, weaving together the values of sentiment and intellect. This poetic intention includes both poems that were published in 1773 and those that remained unpublished but were circulated in the intimacy of the Warrington circle. At times these poems were also circulated in manuscript in the wider network of the Dissenting community. Anna Aikin's praise of Joseph Priestley's wife, Mary Wilkinson Priestley, encapsulates Aikin's ideal of the balance of mind and feeling: 'So cool a judgment, and a heart so warm' (*PALB* 1, l. 26). When visiting the Priestleys at home,

> Oft have I there the social circle joined
> Whose brightening influence raised my pensive mind,
> For none within that circle's magic bound,
> But sprightly spirits move their chearful round.

> *(PALB 2, ll. 41–4)*

Aikin praises the individual autonomy and group cohesion of the members of the 'social circle': they are not 'bound' by a charm, but shaped through voluntary association, and notably, though ornamented by 'easy smiles', no 'dark unfriendly passions enter there' (*PALB* 2, l. 46). The principle connects sociality and morality: it is 'ev'ry social tye that binds the good' (*PALB* 18, l. 40). In his pedagogic experiments at the Academy, her father had fostered a set of informal 'societies', urging tutors and students voluntarily to join associations to help them with elocution and composition.[16] This sense of freedom within propriety structures many of Anna Aikin's images, and in her poems she often claims both the desirability of boundaries, and their elasticity. For example, in 'On a Lady's Writing', the Lady's writing is praised for being 'Correct though free, and regular though fair' (*PALB* 70, l. 4). In these poems of her twenties, during which time Anna published all but twenty-two poems of her entire lifetime œuvre, there is hardly any reference to 'passion' or any extreme emotions. Instead, she braids the sociable and the pedagogic together into the notion of 'friendship' – that informal polite manner that allows rational discourse to take place, and for it to wander between the study and the garden, assimilating domestic affection and mental exercise, and apparently drawing women and men together within the circle. This ideal was, of course, not singular to Warrington; it formed part of a more general movement of middle-class consolidation through the promotion of a coherent ideology of polite manners.[17] And its companion was the concourse of 'polite letters'. A letter from Elizabeth Montagu to Anna Aikin defines the effect of polite letters to 'inspire candour, a social spirit, and gentle manners; to teach a disdain of frivolous amusements, injurious censoriousness, and foolish animosities'.[18] In the freedom of this particular community, with its intimate ties of family, religion, and aspiration, we find an exemplary site of such an ideal, and one in which the differences between men and women, though evident enough to us, might have appeared to Aikin herself as benevolently robed in a universal, enlightened, non-gendered version of selfhood.

In a genealogy of literary sociability, we might locate in Warrington a precursor to the early twentieth-century Bloomsbury intelligentsia, whose convergence of male Cambridge education with the Stephens daughters' accomplishments and talents also strove towards a rigorous intellectual life, both polite and informal. As Priestley later recalled of the Warrington group's teas: 'our conversation was equally instructive and pleasing.'[19] In a poem addressed to William Enfield, tutor of Belles Lettres and Rector Academiae from 1770, Anna Aikin presents a rule of pedagogy based on 'the friendly heart' (*PALB* 68, l. 1). She reminds Enfield to 'cease the task by precept to inform' (*PALB* 68, l. 8), since it is an intrinsic amiability that will better do the job: 'Thy candid manners and thy active mind / With more prevailing force the will shall bind' (*PALB* 68, ll. 10–11). Friendship not only links feeling with mind, it 'better than a Muse inspires' (*PALB* 6, l. 4). So we can say that, if Anna Aikin unselfconsciously wrote the poetry of sensibility, it was in part because its very norms were formulated at her home. If she disregarded the need for women's education, it was because the kind of domesticity she lived within encouraged female intellectual endeavour. What may seem conventional was, paradoxically, an original convention, quite different from the convention of originality that saturated so much poetry of the 1790s, and that we think of as Romantic.

Yet the freedoms of the world that enveloped Anna Aikin were also its limitations. The voluntary links of sociability were not only grounded in the familial, social, and religious links that bind the community together, but reliant upon those bindings. When, in the later 1780s and early 1790s, Anna Barbauld found herself in the more perilously open voluntary associations of radical London, she also found within herself a freer though perhaps less sonorous voice, one grounded in a set of premisses that had always to be debated, and never taken for granted.

A pair of poems called 'Characters' in the 1773 *Poems* suggest something of this limitation: they praise the balance of the women described, but both also turn on the idea of 'excess' – that moment when goodness may move into something that breaks bounds: 'Her charity almost becomes excess' (*PALB* 64, l. 12). These poems are only two of a much larger number of unpublished depictions of friends – poems that shift under our gaze from being portraits of those in Anna Aikin's circle (the ones above addressed to women who both become sisters-in-law, Susannah Barbauld and Martha Jennings) to personifying more general axioms of conduct in polite society. The sequence of more than ten poems offers an innovative and generically distinct type of poem, sketches of members of a provincial social circle, written in a tone that is both intimate and restrained. The set of three to Mrs Rigby and her two daughters (both reputed to be Warrington heart-breakers) recapitulate Aikin's play with liberty and restraint, intention and excess. The mother Sarah Taylor Rigby is 'Prudent, tho' gay and active, yet serene' (*PALB* 65, l. 9), whilst her daughter Sarah Rigby is more of a flirt, endowed with 'pensive languorous, mixed with sprightly ease, / And graceful pride, and manners form'd to please' (*PALB* 66, ll. 5–6). Least tamed is Elizabeth Rigby, who is not yet able to master her own charm: 'Her careless eyes with quick unsettled glance / At random shoot their fires and wound by chance' (*PALB* 66, ll. 7–8).

In these poems, Aikin presents her own voice as slightly superior to those she is depicting; in others of the 'Characters', her voice is that of an admirer, a student, and a peer. They suggest that Barbauld's youthful poetic career was both bounded and authorized by her role as a privileged daughter and sister. Her brother was instrumental in the publication of her 1773 *Poems*, and he took over a paternal role after the death of their father. Although he was four years younger than his sister, he assumed an authoritative position. When he returned to Warrington after finishing his medical studies in Aberdeen, 'by his persuasion and assistance her Poems were selected, revised, and arranged for publication . . . Like the parent bird who pushes off its young to their first flight, he procured the paper, and set the press to work on his own authority.'[20] Looking over the whole of Anna's life, when she was an Aikin as well as when she married and was a Barbauld, we see that, except for the years when John Aikin practised medicine in Yarmouth, he was a near-present influence and may at times have even been something of a burden to her. He himself wished to be recognized as a 'polite writer and cultivator of elegant literature', yet he was far less successful than his sister.[21] A volume of essays, *Evenings at Home* (published shortly after Anna's 1773 *Poems*), included essays by both brother and sister. When Charles James Fox complimented John Aikin on various essays in the joint volume, Aikin had to answer to each one mentioned, 'That is my sister's', until, Samuel Rogers writes in his *Table Talk*, 'Fox thought it best to say no more about the book'.[22] John's daughter, Lucy Aikin, depicts the relationship as a 'literary partnership', but a recurring motif in her memoir of both her father and Anna is Lucy's suggestion that John Aikin has been undervalued in a world that spends too much time crediting his sister. There is a quality to their interdependence that suggests a reversal of the relationship between William and Dorothy Wordsworth; while it was William who was the successful poet and Dorothy his dependant, the complex symbiosis of brother and sister is striking.

The appearance of the 1773 *Poems* was beneficial both for the Warrington Academy and for Anna Aikin. William Woodfall's discussion of the *Poems* in the *Monthly Review* reminds its readers of Aikin's place within the informal familial-pedagogic network of Dissenting intellectuals, suggesting her indebted-

ness to her social circle: 'The pupils of that very useful seminar
[Warrington] ... celebrated her genius, and diffused her
praises far and wide; and some of her compositions have been
read and admired by persons of the first taste and judgment in
the republic of letters.'[23] The volume signalled a step away
from the world of the private circulation of poems into a public
print culture. But, if Warrington gave fame to Anna Aikin, the
volume also promoted the Academy. One of the best poems of
the volume, 'The Invitation', serves as an advertisement for the
institution, describing its pedagogic aims: 'Beneath [the Mer-
sey's] willows rove th'inquiring youth / And court the fair
majestic form of truth', picturing its pleasant surrounds: 'Here
bath'd by frequent show'rs cool vales are seen, / Cloath'd with
fresh verdure, and eternal green'; and enacting its polite
rhetoric: 'Where science smiles, the Muses join the train; / And
gentlest arts and purest manners reign' (*SPP* 53, ll. 95–6,
109–10, 51, ll. 55–6). John Guillory has shown how Anna
Aikin's landscape poetry participates (however unselfconsciously) in the project of cultural advancement by Dissenters
through taking on and forward 'polite vernacular discourse',
suggesting that 'cultural can be acquired like property'.[24] That
is, while the aristocracy claimed its position by antiquity and
entitlement, the bourgeoisie might buy it, and not only as a
welter of objects but also through education, taste, and
sensibility. It was good publicity for the Academy that in the
1775 *Annual Register* David Garrick had noted that Anna Aikin
'lately sung the sweetest lay'.[25]

'The Invitation' is a meditative iambic pentameter loco-
description that distils the benevolence of the Warrington
ethos, evincing the delights and accomplishments of the
Warrington Academy itself. To take the measure of its self-
confident self-portrait against her more critical later poetry,
written when she was Mrs Barbauld, it is worth returning to a
comparison with her late poem, *Eighteen Hundred and Eleven*.
'The Invitation' projects forward from 1772 a future in which
the Corporation and Test Acts have been repealed, and the
students of Warrington fully integrated into civil society.
Realizing their youthful ambitions, they are called by their
country, 'To fix her laws, her spirit to sustain, / And light up
glory thro' her wide domain!' (*SPP* 54, ll. 137–8). 'The

Invitation' appears quite naive next to the dystopic view of London in ruins in *Eighteen Hundred and Eleven*, a poem that investigates and aims to make sense of the dialectics of empire and commerce, where 'Arts, arms and wealth destroy the fruits they bring' (*SPP* 173, l. 315).[26]

But publicity is one thing, lived experience another, and against Anna Aikin's prospectus for Warrington we need to place the hints from the Academy's papers that life there was actually very fraught. Henry Bright, a nineteenth-century Lancashire historian, found documents amongst the papers of the Academy's founder John Seddon that attest to ongoing emotional and financial tumult. Love affairs begun with the daughters of tutors, rowdy nights in local taverns, and bad behaviour by students who could not be properly disciplined because the Academy feared losing their fees meant that the Warrington Academy was in a continual state of psychological and financial difficulty. Aikin's amusing portraits of the flirtatious Rigby girls make a strong counterpoint to the report that: 'The beautiful Miss Rigbys made wild work with the students' hearts; and the trustees had to insist that they must be removed from the house if any students stayed there.' A memorandum from Gilbert Wakefield suggests the problem: 'The Academy is neither school nor college; it is without the supervision exercised in the one, and it wants the influence and authority of the other, – the students are treated as men, while they are but a set of wild and reckless boys.'[27]

So, when William Woodfall in the *Monthly Review* criticized the *Poems* of 1773 for lacking 'passion', he may have identified not a poetic fault but a useful strategy.[28] The problem is not that Barbauld's poetic is unfeminine, and 'cold', as Coleridge would scurrilously declare many years later; but that the amiable sociability upon which Warrington was built had to be made rhetorically firm so as not to call attention to the troubles of a small community that had no 'real sanctions against bad behaviour, except expulsion', which it was financially difficult to enforce.[29] This is what Lucy Aikin later called Warrington's 'long struggle against [the finally] incurable disease' of operating in a buyer's educational market.[30] So, though Anna Aikin's Warrington poetry does perhaps exhibit, as William McCarthy suggests, a defence against passion, this is in keeping with a poetry that is fundamentally aiming at assimilation, not at subversion.[31]

Aikin is very good at gentle satire, as her 'Mouse's Petition' exemplifies: it makes fun of the freedom-loving Priestley for keeping a mouse caged for scientific experimentation. Aikin ventriloquizes the plaintive mouse:

> If e'er thy breath with freedom glow'd,
> And spurned a tyrant's chain,
> Let not thy strong oppressive force
> A free-born mouse detain.
>
> (*SPP* 71, ll. 9–12)

In her Warrington poetry, Anna Aikin displays the good poetic manners of a sister and daughter, endorsing the sexual division of intellectual labour that paradoxically unites the Aikin family enterprise: to her brother she writes, 'To thee, the flute and sounding lyre decreed, / Mine, the low murmurs of the tuneful reed' (*PALB* 19, ll. 92–3).

Amongst the Warrington poems, 'A Summer Evening's Meditation' is the strongest, and it offers suggestions of an autonomy beyond what even the elasticity of Warrington boundaries will allow. The speaker experiences the freedoms offered by thought, by using her reason to think about the evening and the sky and the larger universe. She sees the night sky illuminated by the celestial prospect, which opens her intellectual imagination; 'This dead of midnight is the noon of thought, / And wisdom mounts her zenith with the stars' (*SPP* 100, ll. 51–2). The speaker lets her mind soar way above and beyond her vernal surroundings, where 'I launch into the trackless deeps of space' (*SPP* 100, l. 82), exploring the farthest extent of the universe. As she moves outwards, something inside moves as well, the 'self-collected soul' (*SPP* 100, l. 53) begins its own ascent, out beyond what she can see to what she can only imagine, stopped only by the sublimity of the experience itself, where 'thought astonish'd stops her bold career.' (*SPP* 101, l. 98) This 'soul' is a very human soul; or rather, it is a version of the human as god-like – the speaker finds within herself that spark of energy that is the imagination. This experience of the intellectual

25

imagination is brought down to earth again, circumscribed by 'the known accustom'd spot' of Warrington until

> the hour will come
> When all these splendours bursting on my sight
> Shall stand unveil'd, and to my ravish'd sense
> Unlock the glories of the world unknown.

(SPP 102, ll. 119–22)

Her glimpses of this as yet inchoate world comes to her through what she has learned of science and the political discourse of liberation, and she experiences it as a sequence of *feelings*, the psychology of bodily reaction theorized by Hartley and made into the poetry of sensibility.

This voice of feeling will grow stronger as Anna Aikin, now the married Mrs Barbauld, comes to know more about the passions of both politics and domesticity, and as her writing comes to be built from that passionate knowledge. As we shall see, her political understanding was both sharpened and concretized in the urban milieu of 1780s and early 1790s radical London, where the abstractions of Warrington were brought to bear on actual political events and decisions. And her husband Rochemont Barbauld's developing madness, which ended in his estrangement from his wife and his subsequent suicide, made visible to her the interior vistas of violent eccentricity. The reality of a world as yet unknown would come to be seen by many of Barbauld's peers as immanent in the material apocalypse of the French Revolution. If the *Poems* of 1773 poetically publicized the familiarity of Warrington, the volume nonetheless drew Anna Aikin out towards that glorious world that would allow her both anonymity and autonomy, and into the world of writers associated with the London publisher Joseph Johnson.

MARY ROBINSON: A POET OF SENSIBILITY

There is something both charming and appalling about the 30-year-old Anna Barbauld's apparent self-confidence and lack of self-consciousness. And her assets and limitations become palpable and disturbing when set against her younger acolyte,

Mary Robinson, in whom self-consciousness was necessary as a method of survival. As I suggested in Chapter 1, Anna Barbauld begins to look like Emma Woodhouse when we approach Mary Robinson, a poet of extremity, in equal parts ruthless, passionate, sentimental, and always self-reliant. Though Robinson's first volume is less impressive poetically than Barbauld's, her achievement in producing it is rather more magnificent. Robinson had no first-hand experience of a similar environment, yet her 1775 *Poems* draws on and conforms exactly to the range of conventions associated with the values of virtue and empathy and polite sociability that permeated Warrington. It is not surprising that she held Anna Barbauld up as a literary model and saw her own entry into poetic vocation as linked to Barbauld's.

Robinson placed herself in a poetic tradition in which her own access to her vocation was catalysed by reading the older poet's 1773 *Poems*. With this in mind, we can see ways in which Robinson's volume imitates Barbauld's in both content and form. A few of the poems are directly inspired by or imitate Barbauld's work. She reworks the amusing and satiric poem 'The Mouse's Petition' as 'The Linnet's Petition', but the transformation results in a heavy sentimentality instead of wit. The achievement of Barbauld's poem is that it mingles its political point about freedom with its teasing point about Priestley, presented through the example of the Rights of Vermin. Robinson picks the conventional symbol of freedom, a bird, and produces the political point in a sentimentalized manner. There is no movement in the poem: Robinson's poems share the generic conventions rather than the particular combination of wit and restraint that characterizes much of Barbauld's work.

Through her emulation of Barbauld, however, we can learn something about Robinson's aspiration as a poet. Robinson wants to reproduce the sense of sociable familiarity that lies at the core of Warrington poetics. But where Barbauld's volume is saturated with an easy and entitled sense of connection and friendship, Robinson's poems struggle to assure us that she is socially implanted; half of the poems in her first volume are either addressed to or are about a 'Friend'. Robinson mirrors Barbauld's poetic portraits of 'Characters', in three poems of the same title: she reiterates Anna's praise of poise – 'Sprightly, yet wise, and witty, though sedate' (*P.* 35, l. 6) – but without the edge or difficulty that propels the motive of Anna's examples.

The question raised by these strangely impersonal poems of intimacy is whether Robinson has converted into poetic simulacra – waxwork replicas – what was *actually experienced* by the young Barbauld. And, if this is the case, what does that mean for making sense of and passing judgement on her poems? In 1800, at the end of her life, Robinson would still be craving that intimate circle of intellectual friends that she partially invents in her first volume. Judith Pascoe, the foremost scholar and editor of Robinson's poetry, calls our attention to this yearning in a letter Robinson wrote in September 1800: 'Oh! Heavens! If a Select Society could be formed . . . a world of Talents, drawn into a small but brilliant circle, – what a splendid Sunshine would it display' (*SP* 43). While Barbauld assumed her own status and security in the world, and so rarely had to *reflect* upon it, Mary Robinson was always producing meta-commentaries about herself, in part to establish herself as she wished to be.

At the same time, however, it is important to note that the young Barbauld is not the only poet Robinson imitates. Robinson finds her own fullest voice and her coherent poetic identity as an urban Romantic poet – her talents requiring a liberal metropolitan environment to fuel her vast intellectual and social energies. Her later work includes poems of extraordinary power that show how much more she was herself within the new genres of late-eighteenth-century Romanticism rather than the conventions of restrained sensibility. But Robinson put herself through a poetic education that started in the vocational tradition of beginning with imitations of the ancients, and her first volume of verse is articulated almost entirely in the conventional rhetoric of the contrast between city and country. This includes poems that exalt the idea of meditative retreat from the confusion of the city, as well as comic poems inhabited by stock pastoral shepherds and shepherdesses, wittily enlivened for the knowing self-conscious poet and reader by their artful presentation of unaffected straightforwardness:

> But alas! t'other day at the fair,
> (Sad story for me to relate,)
> He bought ribbons for Phillis's hair,
> For Phillis, the nymph that I hate.

(P. 2, ll. 1–4)

Robinson works the stylish and satirical end of this contrast as well: her 'Letter to a Friend on Leaving Town' draws on Alexander Pope's urban poetics, and imitating his balanced yet individual couplet, embeds this comedy within an overall poetic of rural retreat:

> Scandal and coffee, pass the morn away,
> At night a rout, an opera or a play;
> Thus glide their life, partly through inclination,
> Yet more, because it is the reigning fashion.
> .   .   .   .   .   .
> Henceforth, retirement, is my chosen seat,
> Far from the insolent, the vain, the great,
> Sweet solitude, ah! Welcome to my breast,
> And with thee welcome, sweet content and rest.

(SP 73, ll. 41–4; 74, ll. 71–4)

Robinson's 1775 volume as a whole weaves together bits of mid-century wit, the later, more benign conventions of Aikin's 'free familiar conversation' and those used by other poets of sensibility, along with movement towards the meditative-visionary poetry of the end of the century. The *Oracle* would define her talent as breathing 'The tender Strain of SAPPHO with the soft pathetic Melancholy of Collins' (29 July 1789, 3). Judith Pascoe remarks also on Robinson's indebtedness to the 'graveyard' poets such as Gray and Edward Young, in addition to Cowper and Akenside (*SP* 48).

These poems inform us that from early on one of Mary Robinson's greatest talents was her facility for imitation. We know from her reputation as an actress working with Garrick and Sheridan that she had a genius for becoming her roles on stage. When we look at her poetic œuvre over twenty years, we might imagine her as the model for what Keats would later call the chameleon poet who 'has no Identity; he is continually informing and filling some other Body'. But, though Keats meant that the excellence of a poet could be described as a

29

function of his or her ability so to empathize with his or her creations that the boundaries of the poet's self become permeable to the imagined *being*, it is sometimes the case with Robinson that her chameleon capacity is that of filling in for 'some other' *poet*'s voice. This may appear to be a harsh criticism, particularly in the light of the Romantic criterion (one that still operates today) that poetic excellence can be directly measured by the sincerity and expressive truth of a poet's work. But in the act of poetic imitation Robinson is able to assert her place in a long and important tradition of poetic making as the art of imitation with variation. The self-confidence necessary for the apprenticeship of the poet – alone in the company of powerful foreparents – is usually associated with male poets, and, according to Walter Jackson Bate, the burden of the poetic past was felt particularly strongly in the eighteenth century. He argues that this 'burden of the past' was faced first by poets foregrounding the arts of imitation: 'never before and never thus far since have the use and imitation of past models (classical or other) been more sustained, more thoughtful, more brilliant.'[32] We can admire Robinson's ambitious sense of poetic vocation at the age of 16. And this sort of poetic fearlessness is evident throughout Robinson's œuvre. It is evident as well in the determined way in which she went about mastering the world around her through an unwavering confidence in her own capacity to act and write and work to support herself and her daughter in an often chaotic life.

When looking at Robinson's first volume it is also important to bear in mind that working within poetic convention was the habit of the mid-eighteenth century, a habit that was altered by individuals such as the young Anna Barbauld by their striking formulations and irrepressible personal voice, a habit that ultimately broke through the internal logic of sensibility itself. The poetics of sensibility sought to establish and represent ever-greater depths of empathy – both towards the subjects they imagined and towards the reader. But to register the value of empathy and to prove its authenticity, both the personality and sensibility of the poet became ever more important to poetic purpose more generally. It is possible to trace through Robinson's poetic career some of the stages in the history of eighteenth-century poetry as it shifts from sensibility to Romanticism. If we invoke sensibility's early criteria of politeness and sympathy, we will make very different judgements on her work than if we invoke the later eighteenth-century Romantic principles of originality and sincerity.

Much of the polish of Anna Barbauld's poetry derives from her security in the world, which paradoxically carries with it a kind of buffer against interior exploration and self-knowledge. Robinson's gift for mimicry and her desire to appropriate the poetic persona of the Woman of Letters offered her a way of masking some of her own painful psychological deficits. She may do an excellent job of appealing to the same sociable values as Aikin, but her personal life and her childhood had been far less secure than those of Revd. Aikin's daughter.

Given the strength of its self-presentation as an envoy from the world of polite letters, it comes as something of a shock to learn that Robinson's 1775 *Poems* appeared while she was living in the Fleet Prison in London with her infant daughter and her husband of two years, Thomas Robinson, a man who lied and gambled and womanized, and whose excessive debts pulled them out of Hatton Garden into gaol. Thomas Robinson lived as a pleasure-seeker without worrying about the means to support his habit and he introduced his 15-year-old bride to the pleasures and penalties of excess. Robinson was the natural son of a Welsh gentleman, and he associated in London with libertine aristocrats. Important among these companions was George, Lord Lyttleton, who appealed to Thomas Robinson because he drank and gambled and to Mary Darby Robinson because he was an accomplished poet and reader of poetry, and something of a philosopher. It was said of him that he went to the tavern with a 'whore in his hand and a Horace in his pocket'.[33]

In fact, it was Lyttleton who had given Anna Aikin's *Poems* to Robinson in 1773. Aikin, no doubt, would have been appalled to find that the volume was a prop used by Lyttleton to seduce the young bride, as Robinson accuses him of doing in her *Memoirs*. Known to Walpole as having his own 'style of lovemaking', Lyttleton was political, poetical, and libertine.[34] The world from which he emerged was the urban privileged aristocracy. He was attracted to intellectual women, and he

31

was rumoured to have had an affair with the bluestocking Elizabeth Montagu (who, I noted earlier, had asked Anna Aikin to start a women's academy of learning). Given the disorder of Robinson's life in her mid-adolescence, it may be, ironically, that Robinson's address to Lyttleton is one of the volume's most genuine addresses to a friend. Her attachment to poetic convention in the volume, contradictory though it may appear, was a necessary element of personal authenticity for Robinson – a mode of defence against the realities of her fraught personal relationships, and an image of how her life might be more genuine. Robinson is authentically inauthentic, and never more so than when she protests her sincerity:

> I always SPEAK what I BELIEVE;
> I know not if I CAN deceive;
> Because I NEVER TRIED.

> (*SP* 140, ll. 46–8)

If 'A Summer's Evening Meditation' is Aikin's strongest poem in her first volume, the penultimate poem of Robinson's 1775 *Poems*, 'The Vision', occupies a similar position in the volume and aims for a similar effect. Though neither poem is precisely an *ars poetica*, both include a forceful invocation of the powers of the fancy and imagination to raise the poetic speakers beyond the limits of their worlds, and glimpse another way of being and knowing.

Anna Aikin's poem is one of the most impressive instances of what M. H. Abrams analysed and named 'the Greater Romantic Ode' – a place-descriptive poem in which the poetic self surveys the scene around her, then probes inwards until, like a mobius-strip, her inner self meets up with the outer world through the imaginative encounter between subjectivity and the world of objects. Mary Robinson's poem is not as subtly made, nor as psychologically complex, but in 'The Vision' she aims to make a place for the workings of her identity as poet, and links the making of poetry with the large category that underpins so much of the poetry of sensibility, Virtue. Virtue is the intersection for her of 'peace, humility, and love' (*P*. 119, l. 23). The limits set in Aikin's world are those of place – her fantasy exploration of a new world draws on metaphors of travel, infinitude, and expansion. For Robinson, the limits are set by a world of pleasure and inconsequent joy. Her reverie in 'a lonely shade / For meditation and contentment made' (*P.* 118, l. 2) takes her away from the superficialities of her usual urban surrounds to 'the real pleasures of an honest mind' (*P.* 122, l. 68). Her poetic persona is clarified in this poem – she aims to produce herself as an intellectual struggling against the hollow world around her.

GROWING UP IN BRISTOL AND LONDON

How did this 15-year-old young woman end up in prison with a ne'er-do-well husband, an infant child, and a manuscript of poems? The amount of documentation about Anna Barbauld's youth is vast by comparison with Robinson's, but there is little beyond Barbauld's fairly reticent letters that offer her own accounting of herself. The textual evidence for Mary Robinson's experience of youth can be found primarily in her 1775 *Poems* and in her memory of her childhood as recorded in her *Memoirs*. Robinson began writing her *Memoirs* in 1798, when she was 40 years old, and the idiom she drew on reflected twenty-five years of changes in literary fashion. While Anna Barbauld's personal history was always narrated as part of a family story, embedded within memoirs of her father and her brother and herself by niece and great-niece, in which Barbauld herself was the object of the narration, Mary Robinson had to write the story herself, which gave her greater room for improvement, less room for the test of corroboration. If the poems in the 1775 volume are steeped in the rhetoric of polite sociability, the *Memoirs* of 1798 describe Robinson's youth in the language of Romantic solitude amidst a rural landscape of ruins.

Like the young Anna Barbauld, Robinson presents herself as a precocious child, but she narrates this along Gothic rather than Deist lines. In her *Memoirs*, sociability as a desideratum has given way to solitude as an index of authorial honesty, and the first memories presented are those of the child Mary Darby sitting alone in the Gothic ruins of the Minster House in Bristol where she was born on 27 November 1758: 'A spot more calculated to inspire the soul with mournful meditation can

33

scarcely be found amidst the monuments of antiquity' (*Per*. 17). So conventions of Romanticism are added to the changes memory makes on immediate experience as the ailing mature woman redraws her infancy. Yet this image of Mary Darby's sense of isolation reflected in her environs probably gives a more accurate rendering of her earliest emotional experiences than do the sociable poetics she drew on in the 1775 volume.

Robinson makes more sense as a Romantic figure than a 'polite' one, because, although she would travel in social circles as a 'leader of the ton', her origins, her failed marriage, her acting career, and her sexual affairs prevented her from ever being considered truly 'genteel'. Robinson was always precariously placed, *in* but not *of* polite (and not so polite) society. One commentator remarked that guests invited to her home in Berkeley Square, where she lived through the 1790s, found 'her manners and conversation ... to want refinement and decorum'.[35] A century later *The Dictionary of National Biography* would call her 'vain, ostentatious, fond of exhibiting herself, and wanting in refinement'.

The psychological truth was that Mary Darby lived an unstable life in a financially and personally disintegrating family. She recalled her father, Nicholas Darby, as a man of 'strong mind, high spirit, and great personal intrepidity' (*Per*. 18). Robinson establishes courage as a family trait inherited through her father's line, and she also makes a claim to the Enlightenment and intellectual tradition through her mother, who was related to John Locke. In her *Memoir*, Robinson recalls her earliest childhood as happy in a prosperous family situation, but she also suggests that ill omens shadowed her birth: at the very hour she was born,

> The wind whistled round the dark pinnacles of the minster tower, and the rain beat in torrents against the casements of her [mother's] chamber. Through life the tempest has followed my footsteps; and I have in vain looked for a short interval of repose from the perseverance of sorrow. (*Per*. 18)

In 1765, when Mary was 7 years old, her father went to the south coast of Labrador to build a whale fishery. His wife, Hester Darby, did not go with him, and she later learned that Nicholas Darby had taken a mistress with him. From that time forward he never lived again with his wife and children, though he reappeared from time to time to issue rules and regulations about how they were to behave. The gap between his own behaviour and what he expected of his family seems not to have been visible to his own eyes, though we might speculate that it had an effect on the young Mary Darby. Her recollections suggest a rift within her between a deepening sense of personal interiority and a distanced external world in which she had to live. Her memory of that interior self gives early intimations of her own poetic vocation: for example, while listening to the choristers singing:

> I can at this moment recall to memory the sensations I then experienced; the tones that seemed to thrill through my heart, the longing that I felt to unite my feeble voice to the full anthem, and the awful though sublime impression which the church service never failed to make upon my feelings. (*Per.* 21)

The Labrador episode financially ruined Nicholas Darby, and in 1768, when Mary was 10 years old, the family's property was auctioned, and mother and children moved to Chelsea, then a suburb on the edge of London, where Mary was sent to a succession of schools. In the *Memoirs*, Robinson suggests that she had a superior early education, and in the charming and comic 'Picture of my Mind' she writes:

> My FAULTS I OWN – my VIRTUES KNOW;
> To EDUCATION half I owe,
> And NATURE did the rest.

> (*SP* 140, ll. 40–2)

It seems that Mary Darby saw her education as her principle of continuity and security, in which the world was predictable, and where she could exert some control. In Bristol she was taught in the school maintained by Hannah More's sisters, and in Chelsea she was taught by a redoubtable teacher, Meribah Lorrington, who introduced Mary Darby to the pleasures of the intellect: 'All that I ever learned I acquired from this extraordinary woman' (*Per.* 29). It was in that school that Darby began to write poetry. Some of these poems, written when she 'was between twelve and thirteen years of age', were included in the 1775 volume. From an early age, then, Darby saw herself as belonging to a sorority of intellectual women. And, while Anna Barbauld was considered to be one amongst equals in the bluestocking set, a place she never particularly wished to inhabit, Mary Robinson aspired always to that status, without being welcomed in. What family was to Anna Aikin, the world of books and female intellectual models was to Mary Darby.

In one of the periods when Nicholas Darby had cut off all contact with the family, Hester Darby set up her own school in London, in which Mary became the literature mistress. But, when Nicholas showed up, he demanded that the school be closed down. Nicholas Darby was extremely concerned with seemliness and propriety, perhaps as a foil to his messy personal life and the uncertainty of his financial situation. Whereas Anna Aikin stayed home being a good daughter until Rochemont Barbauld took her away to a new home where she then became a good wife, dislocation was a constant theme of Mary Darby Robinson's early life. The situation of a lone mother travelling with children back and forth from Bristol to London, Chelsea to Marylebone to Chancery Lane, and an estranged father going back and forth across the Atlantic is not uncharacteristic of late-eighteenth-century England as a place of increased mobility, with London at the centre of a hub of radiating global links. As Mary Darby's world became less and less coherent, she built up a stronger sense of an interior self, a sense of identity as founded within the self, rather than from her relation to environment, place, or family connection. The young Darby is thus much more of an incipiently romantic personality than was the young Anna Aikin. Robinson's is a self-making and self-reliant identity, while Aikin's is more at ease and compliant. In these affective responses to their environments, we catch the difference between being born in 1743 and in 1758.

While practising her poetic skills, Mary Darby also embarked on her acting career. The link between poetry and acting came through Mary's love of both reading and writing: 'My early love for lyric harmony had led me to a fondness for the more sublime scenes of dramatic poetry' (*Per.* 34). She memorized and performed some famous speeches from Shakespeare's plays, and the headmistress of the last school she attended brought her to the attention of John Hussey, the ballet master at Covent Garden. Then a series of connections got Mary Darby an introduction to the ageing, but charismatic and extremely influential David Garrick, who was then the manager of the Drury Lane theatre. At 14, she recited speeches from Nicholas Rowe's *Jane Shore* and Garrick decided to put her on as Cordelia, opposite his own Lear. Just before she was to make her debut, however, she was approached by and then engaged and married to Thomas Robinson.

This must have presented itself as a better option to her mother than letting her child go on the stage. The marriage was not a love match. The Darby family situation was even more difficult than usual. Mary's brother George was ill with smallpox, and, although he recovered, Mary then caught the illness herself and Thomas Robinson, who had played a central part in helping Hester Darby deal with the necessaries of George's illness and recovery, now turned all his attention to Mary. When Robinson approached Hester to ask to marry her daughter, the arrangements were quickly made and carried out. She was only 'a few months advanced in my sixteenth year' (*Per.* 41) and married. Robinson's memories of the occasion of the wedding are interesting. She pays lots of attention to her dress – in fact throughout the *Memoirs* she always keeps us in mind of how she appeared; she was very well aware of how dress can shape the reactions to personality, and how dress is a kind of mask that one can don to project a kind of identity. She tells us that she 'dressed in the habit of a quaker' (*Per.* 43) for the event, suggesting the importance of appearing modest and honest and unadorned, but also suggesting as well the aspect of the event that was dissenting – her dress serves as a metaphor for her dissent from the marriage itself. In fact, Thomas Robinson had insisted upon a clandestine marriage, and had convinced Hester Darby both that he was due a large inheritance and land, and that the marriage had to be kept secret to ensure the completion of his articles with the solicitor John Vernon (*Per.* 37). In reality he was not an heir to a large fortune but rather an illegitimate son, filled with rage about how fortune had dealt with him, and when he and his new wife returned to London, he resolved to behave as if he were an heir, even though he had no resources to fund his high life.

It was in this period that Mary Robinson began the central discipline of her life: maintaining herself and her dependants in the insecure world of husband, debt, and urban pleasures. Thomas began losing a lot of money at the gambling table and Mary called into service her own skill as a poet: 'My little collection of Poems, which I had arranged for publication, and which had been ready ever since my marriage, I now determined to print immediately' (*Per.* 76). While much of the contemporary public gossip about Mary Robinson figured her as a compromised woman living off wealthy men, in fact she was a determined, if not always successful, breadwinner. When Thomas Robinson was remanded to the King's Bench Prison for thirteen months beginning in May 1775, Mary and their recently born child, Maria Elizabeth, went with him. Mary earned her living there by copying legal documents, just as she earned it by acting when she started her theatrical career in 1776, and as she earned it as the mistress of prominent men. She later earned it as a novelist, as a poet, and as the compiler and editor of the poetry page in the *Morning Post*. Even when she was in debt, Robinson never faltered as a wage-earner, and this accomplishment underlies all her others. She was a woman who got up every morning and went to work. While there might be elements of imitation and posing in her self-presentation and her poetry, she neither minimized nor exaggerated her continuing commitment to her labours. There was enough fecklessness in Nicholas Darby and in Thomas Robinson to ensure that Mary Darby Robinson would protect her dignity and her person through work.

Robinson's 1775 volume was reviewed in the *Monthly Review* as a debut of some interest: 'Though Mrs. Robinson is by no means an Aikin or More, she *sometimes* expresses herself decently enough on her subject.' The quotation next cited in the review encapsulates the psychological motor of Mary Robinson the 'chancer':

> In your own power alone it lies,
> To blend this life with joy, or care,
> Ambition's idle claim despite,
> Think yourself happy; and you are.

(*P*. 115, ll. 44–7)

38

But to be even considered along with Hannah More and Anna Aikin must have been quite thrilling to Mary Robinson. And, on the basis of these comparisons, Robinson sent a copy of the volume to the elegant and controversial Whig, Georgiana, Duchess of Devonshire. This was to lead to a critical change in Robinson's life – her attachment to the Whig aristocracy – and it led, both to her advantage and her trouble, to an affair with the Prince of Wales. Robinson and the Duchess had a somewhat entangled relationship, as both women had affairs with Charles James Fox, both were politically voluble, and both were poets. But Robinson was always a wage-earning poet, and Devonshire always the patroness – an interchange of subordination and emulation drove their relationship. And if Devonshire was in command, nonetheless Robinson had a decisive forceful personality, ironically nicknamed 'Meeky' by Sheridan.[36] As patroness, however, Devonshire was helpful to Mary Robinson, and the list of subscribers to the 1791 volume of *Poems* attests to Devonshire's generosity and genuine appreciation of Robinson's talents. Mary Robinson was heading into the heart of metropolitan society and politics, and its peculiar mix of hedonism and reformism. The times were auspicious for this movement: reform ideology in part interrupted the hierarchy of class society, and made it possible for Robinson to build a vocation and reputation for herself.

In the major poem Mary Robinson wrote while in Fleet Prison, *Captivity, A Poem*, we hear an intimation of where her poetic work and political sympathies might go. For she not only took on menial tasks of copying documents to raise cash for her family; ever industrious, she also worked on a long and important poem.

Published in the autumn of 1777, *Captivity, A Poem; and Celadon, A Tale* works a central theme in the Enlightenment poetics of sensibility: the oppression of persons through slavery and imprisonment, and their capacity for mental freedom: 'whatever punishment the Fates decree / For erring mortals, – still the mind is free' (C. 29). *Captivity* elevates and reworks the prison sentence of Thomas Robinson as an example of oppression (rather than the punishment for excess). *Captivity* raises issues of human rights, and also makes claims for Robinson's poetic vocation through a rhetoric in which she disclaims the very stature that the poem intends. The poem is spoken by a persona who possesses an 'artless breast', singing in 'Nature's unaffected voice' a 'tale which only from Compassion springs' (C. 8). Robinson *was* indeed very young, but in this instance she was able to make an art of artlessness. She presents her husband's debt as ill fortune rather than reckless spending, and the poem cloaks her defence *of* him as compassion *for* him. Robinson's self-awareness is obvious as well in her appeals to the Muse. The poem is Robinson's own in the way it suggests both irony and innocence at the same time: she imagines a reader who will make the kinder judgement upon it:

> Tho' no harmonious Cadence grace the line,
> Nor in each page superior Graces shine,
> Soft pity shall o'er Satire's voice prevail,
> And mild Compassion shall applaud the Tale.

(C. 34)

When she wrote her first volume of verse (as Anna Aikin), Barbauld also employed a rhetoric of diffidence, in particular in relation to her brother, but in her work it produces a very different poetic atmosphere. Aikin's poetic is *naive*, and Robinson's *sentimental*, a distinction made by the German philosopher Schiller in 1795, responding to the varieties of emotion in poetry. The naive poet lives and speaks with an immediacy that can be presented only as lost and desired in the sentimental poet.[37] The sentimental poet, in other words, is always self-aware and longing to be the naive one; while the naive poet knows nothing of these distinctions.

While we can certainly isolate the personal-poetic issue in the rhetoric of *Captivity*, the poem also inhabits the poetic associated with a reform politics, practised by a number of women poets in their work within the abolition movement: Helen Maria Williams, Hannah More, Ann Yearsley, and Anna Barbauld in her 1791 *Epistle to William Wilberforce*.

In Robinson's work, the themes of social compassion and political reform remain constant, but, as she becomes a Romantic poet, she develops a keen ear for the voices of the socially dispossessed. This takes her towards the ethically subtler and socially modest world of the Lake poets. She moves from the opulence of the Whig aristocracy towards middle-class Romantic minimalism. It is not surprising that, like Anna Aikin in her first volume, Robinson offers Friendship as the emblem of meritocratic politics as she invokes a time

> When real worth shall meet with just applause,
> And every bosom glow, in Friendship's cause;
> When every free-born Briton shall revere
> Those sacred Laws to Honor ever dear.

(C. 31)

Anna Aikin and Mary Robinson were engaged in similar poetic activities for entirely different social and psychological reasons and from very different geographical locations. They were both finding their way as practitioners of the arts of poetry, and, over the next fifteen years, both would also discover what were to them the crucial themes and issues to be advanced through their skills. Both would also find themselves involved on the liberal, Whig side of political questions, Aikin as a powerful intellectual presence in the Dissenting reform movement, and Robinson as a woman on the edge of the Whig aristocracy around Fox and the Prince of Wales. Both would find in the French Revolution an energy source of cataclysmic proportions; both would find in the atmosphere of metropolitan radicalism a catalyst to their intellectual development.

3

Actress and Pedagogue: 1774–1789

Over the next fifteen years, both Robinson and Aikin were drawn physically and intellectually into metropolitan life, but they arrived in radical London with very different reputations. For much of the time Mary Robinson was a member of the London *bon ton*, where she was known as a courtesan rather than as a poet; during the same period Anna Aikin (now Anna Barbauld) was immersed in the exhausting routine of teaching small boys in Palgrave, on the border of Norfolk and Suffolk. Neither woman wrote much poetry in these years, but their experiences informed their intellectual and political work through the end of the century. While Mary Robinson was feted for her success as an actress at the Drury Lane theatre, Anna Barbauld was writing *Lessons for Children* of various ages. In her very beautiful *Hymns in Prose for Children* (1781) Barbauld embodies the values and style of Dissenting piety inflected by her particular version of devotional sensibility. At the end of *her* turbulent experiences in the 1780s, Robinson reanimated her poetic vocation through an amphibian rhetoric of louche aristocratic ornament coupled with the new poetic of the Della Cruscans: a sentimental lyricism that used excess in ornamentation as a vehicle for moralizing.

ANNA BARBAULD BETWEEN COUNTRY AND CITY

William Woodfall had lamented the lack of feminine 'passion' and romantic love in Anna Aikin's poems when he reviewed the 1773 volume. But Warrington had not lacked amorous intrigue. Lucy Aikin gives a light and literary account of flourishing romance at the Academy: 'Rousseau's "Heloise", too, had much to answer for, and at its appearance (so Miss Aikin tells me), "everybody instantly fell in love with every body" and then it was that Mr Barbauld won his bride.'[1] Rochemont Barbauld came from a Huguenot family and he was intended for the Established clergy, but he became a Dissenter while at Warrington, and he was one of many students who fell in love with the beautiful Miss Aikin.[2]

A story circulated into the twentieth century that Rochemont would have lost his chance with Anna Aikin if the French revolutionary Jean-Paul Marat had succeeded in *his* suit for her hand. The historian Sidney Phipson showed in the early 1920s that Marat had been employed for a short period of time as the Modern Languages tutor at Warrington before leaving for Oxford, where he robbed the Ashmolean Museum and was subsequently imprisoned in the Bristol Hulks. A former pupil recognized him there as having been the Languages master at Warrington. When Phipson published his argument in *Notes and Queries*, it elicited a reply from a reader, Andrew Ternant, who explained that his father had purchased a Marat pamphlet, later lost, in which were inserted 'two autograph letters addressed to Dr John Aikin [Anna's brother]'. In one of the letters Marat announced 'that his ambition was to become a naturalized Englishman and a suitor for the hand of the doctor's sister (the future Mrs Barbauld)'.[3] The history of not only two people, but also two nations, might have unfolded in unexpected ways if this marriage had taken place. The anecdote makes an interesting counterpoint to Mary Robinson's narrative: for, while a French revolutionary courted the sensible Aikin, Robinson, later a Friend of Liberty, dined and flirted with the Queen of France, and, during the crisis of 1793, wrote a series of poems on Marie-Antoinette's struggles as mother and wife.

Rochemont and Anna were married in 1774, commemorated in a poem in which the bride flirtatiously establishes her hold over Rochemont: he will never be released, 'I my destined captive hold too fast' (*PALB* 90, l. 32). A poem written to Rochemont in 1778, four years later, displays a new awareness of the emotions of interiority:

We'll little care what others do,
And where they go, and what they say;
Our bliss, all inward and our own,
Would only tarnished be, by being shown.

(*SPP* 104, ll. 29–32)

In the light of this poem, we might reconsider Woodfall's review and acknowledge that he did have a point about the earlier untroubled levelness of Anna Aikin's verse. In the intimacy of this poem, the world of manners and social polish is agreeably disturbed by the interior and secret connections of lovers.

Anna Barbauld's energies over the next ten years were devoted to creating a comfortable world for her husband and herself. As they had been in Warrington, her writings were a report on and a public advertisement for her pedagogic/domestic circle and its endeavours. The school for boys at Palgrave, where Rochemont took up his duties as minister, was the financial and intellectual grounding for Barbauld's movements in the world of letters and opinion. In their eleven years at Palgrave Anna became as polished an educationalist as she had been a polite poet at Warrington. Her daily contact with the unguarded emotions of children, in which she observed and experienced the borders between ideas and feelings, is crucial in her writings for children in the 1770s and 1780s. They are grounded in rational assessment of how children learn, but aim to teach the virtuous life by relying on the emotional power of ideas as sensual and lyrical. Her focus on devotional feeling was criticized strongly by her friend and mentor Joseph Priestley when she articulated it in 'Thoughts on the Devotional Taste, on Sects, and on Establishments' (1775). Priestley criticizes her for aligning devotion with 'taste', as if piety were a function of aesthetics; and he is very exercised by her apparent elevation of the irrational aspects of devotion. When she suggests that 'philosophy is unfavourable to piety' and that 'nothing is more prejudicial to the feelings of a devout heart than a habit of disputing on religious subjects', Barbauld seems to be turning her back on the culture of debate that animated Warrington. If someone values religious truth, responds Priestley, they will 'if occasion requires, contend for it

... Did not our Saviour dispute much, St Paul more, the primitive Christians without ceasing, the first reformers and the Puritans the same?'[4] But Barbauld's version of devotion, which animated her *Hymns in Prose for Children* (1781), clearly hit exactly the right note, winning so much public regard that she was held to be the chief pedagogical mentor for the children of the mercantile, aristocratic, and Dissenting elite well into the nineteenth century.

At Palgrave Anna Barbauld continued the Warrington project of blending pedagogy and sociability, but now the circle of adults was narrowed to minister and wife, and now it was Anna who held the keys to the storerooms. The range of responsibilities that she took on included not only teaching and organizing the schedules of the students and the household staff, but also overseeing and maintaining the Palgrave finances. Her husband did not imagine her (at least at the start) as a full teacher but as the housewife who would keep the place running efficiently, both practically and in financial planning, 'tak[ing] upon her the economical part'.[5]

'I will tell you what I have been about,' she writes to her brother in 1775: 'First, then, making up beds; secondly, scolding my maids, preparing for company; and lastly, drawing up and delivering lectures on Geography.' The shift from being daughter to wife entailed a new range of problems and possibilities, and it is worth considering Barbauld's style of devotional sensibility as a way of making sense of the issues and conflicts of domesticity.

The Aikin family still remained a strong cohort, and when the Barbaulds did not have children, Anna turned to her brother John for a solution. After jokingly suggesting in a letter that she expects one of her brother's children, Charles, to be packed 'up in the hamper' and sent to Palgrave, in 1777 she and Rochemont did in fact bring Charles to Palgrave after some serious negotiation with John and his wife, Patsy.

And now, my dear brother and sister, let me again thank you for this precious gift, the value of which we are both more and more sensible of, as we become better acquainted with his sweet disposition and winning manners. As well as a gift, it is a solemn trust, and it shall be our study to fulfill that trust.[6]

The students often came to Palgrave through Aikin–Warrington connections. John Aikin's two sons were pupils, as were the sons of William Enfield, rector at Warrington. Barbauld's beloved Priestley sent his son William, who became a French Citizen in 1792. The father of the feminist Harriet Martineau was educated there. But the reputation of Anna Barbauld drew an ever wider range of pupils, and Palgrave boarded and taught the children of professionals as well as sons of titled families and landed gentry.[7] Although Rochemont Barbauld never included Anna's teaching as part of the authorized work of the school, and did not include the pupils his wife taught when apportioning places and vacancies, her pedagogy was central to the school's curriculum. What were the innovations of the school? McCarthy explains that it was her sympathy with the state of being a child. Barbauld empathized with the difficulties of children and their desire for autonomy and privacy, and their need for intellectual stimulation. Her students remembered her kindly, and one defined her method: she 'broke down the old by rote plans' and made lessons 'more interesting'.[8] The students at Palgrave loved Barbauld's methods: William Taylor described her as 'the mother of [his] mind', and Lucy Aikin reported that Thomas Denman, Lord Chancellor in 1832, 'cherishes her memory most religiously. In a great public entertainment where I saw him last year, he came up and said with a look of delight, "I dreamed of Mrs Barbauld only last night"!'[9]

Barbauld lectured in geography and history, and gave the children lots of practice in reciting aloud, acting in plays, and writing verse. In a letter to her brother in 1775, she informs him, 'The Palgrave Seminary will soon abound with poets, even as the green fields abound with grasshoppers.'[10] But she did not return to the poetry that had won her reputation: 'You are very favourable to my fragments; – fragments, however, they are like to continue unless I had a little more time.' William Turner's 1825 memorial article notes that 'during this whole period [1774–85] her muse did not favour the public with any of her productions; although some exquisite gems were occasionally dug from the poetic vein'.[11] As at Warrington, much of her poetry of this period is occasional, and her attention focuses on the schoolboys she was dealing with daily.

Her poems were meant to be read and recited by her pupils, such as the gently deflating 'Written on a Marble', which reduces the struggle for global domination to a boy's game of marbles: 'Your heroes are overgrown schoolboys / Who scuffle for empires and toys' (*SPP* 109, ll. 4–5). More charming are the 'Lines to be Spoken by Thomas Denman on the Christmas before his Birthday, When he was Four Years Old': 'I won't be called a baby anymore, / Next February I'm completely four' (*SPP* 108, ll. 3–4).

McCarthy makes the point that Barbauld's pedagogy was aimed as well to make good public speakers and citizens of her charges, in the best traditions of Dissenting intellectualism.[12] Yet we find again the way in which Barbauld's use of that tradition is modified by her aestheticized piety. So she effectively achieved the goal of rhetorical training by harnessing it to her interest in the theatre. She went to the theatre often during these years whenever she was in London, and she bought current plays that were then staged at Palgrave by the pupils. Indeed, the list of play texts at Palgrave shows that amongst them was the ephemeral *Florizel & Perdita*, the adaptation of *The Winter's Tale* that served as the occasion and later the metaphor for Mary Robinson's affair with the Prince Regent.

But it was Barbauld's style, taken into the world through her writings, that gave Palgrave its public standing. Originally written to teach her adopted son, Charles Rochemont Aikin, Barbauld's *Lessons for Children of Two to Three Years Old* (1778), *Lessons for Children of Three Years Old* (1778), and *Lessons for Children from Three to Four Years Old* (1779) were informal and direct, aiming to teach basic skills in logic and comprehension, and to enable children to read by the age of 2. They were in print for generations, as were the widely read *Hymns in Prose for Children* (1781). The hymns are filled with the minute particulars of the world at hand, and they teach observation as inextricable from devotion:

> I have seen the insects sporting in the sun-shine, and darting along the streams; their wings glittered with gold and purple; their bodies shown like the green emerald. (*SPP* 257)

Devotion is learned by *feeling* one's way to God:

Look at the milky way, it is a field of brightness; its pale light is composed of myriads of burning suns.

All of these are God's families; he gives them the sun to shine with a ray of his own glory; he marks the path of the planets, he guides their wanderings through the sky, and traces out their orbit with the finger of his power. (*SPP* 255)

The *Hymns* addresses the deprivations and horrors of the world as well as its beauties, teaching alike by beauty and by fear. Later in the nineteenth century Harriet Martineau recalled: 'In those days we learned Mrs Barbauld's Prose Hymns by heart; and there were parts of them which I dearly loved, but other parts made me shiver with awe.'[13]

All of Barbauld's children's books were published by Joseph Johnson, and he and his changing circle of friends and authors would prove to be an intellectual lifeline for her as she and Rochemont made their winter visits to London over the eleven years of Palgrave work. At Johnson's in the 1770s and early 1780s, the circle was less politically homogeneous than it would come to be in the period after 1788, when presided over by Mary Wollstonecraft, and when allegiances and fallings-out were more frequent in the volatile atmosphere of change abroad. In the Palgrave period, the Barbaulds met through Johnson other educationalists such as Sarah Trimmer, and saw radicals such as Horne Tooke converse with Establishment bishops. Only a few years later, Trimmer would break with the publisher over the partisanship of his author and dinner list.[14] Barbauld described those evenings to her brother in a letter after a trip to London in 1784: 'Our evenings, particularly at Johnson's, were so truly social and lively, that we protracted them sometimes till – but I am not telling tales. Ask – at what time we used to separate.'[15]

Barbauld's *Poems* were reprinted four times in 1773; though she had left Warrington, her reputation was established as a bluestocking and as a new poetic voice as she came into contact with the larger metropolitan intellectual world. We know, for example, that Horace Walpole took Barbauld on a tour of Strawberry Hill, which, in 1790, he recalled with dismay when describing her to a friend as the 'Virago Barbauld'. One excited letter to her brother John Aikin describes the Barbaulds going to see Hannah More's plays, and meeting Elizabeth Montagu, who, not content with being the queen of literature and elegant society, sets up for the queen of fashion and splendour. She is building a very fine house, has a very fine service of plate, dresses and visits more than ever; and I am afraid will be full as much the woman of the world as the philosopher.[16]

Anna Barbauld's standing amongst the women of letters of the later eighteenth century is evinced by her place in Richard Samuel's painting *The Nine Living Muses of Great Britain*, exhibited at the Royal Academy in 1779, where she is painted as one among equals with Elizabeth Carter, Elizabeth Griffith, Angelica Kauffmann, Charlotte Lennox, Catherine Macauley, Elizabeth Montagu, Hannah More, and Hester Thrale, all women who emblematized, for Samuel, the intellectual and artistic capabilities of the English Enlightenment. In her important study of Samuel's painting, Elizabeth Eger makes the point that the image had been widely distributed before its exhibition when published as a print in Johnson's ephemeral 'pocket memorandum' book for 1778. As one of the 'living muses', it seemed to many in the metropolitan intelligentsia that Anna Barbauld the educationalist was not fulfilling the promise of Miss Aikin's *Poems*. Eger's study cites James Barry RA, lamenting Barbauld's provincial existence: '[Barbauld], to the shame and loss of the public, is buried in a retirement at [Palgrave] actually making two-penny books for children; but the appearances may deceive us; some epic or other great work is, I trust, in hand, as the solace of retirement.'[17] Samuel Johnson was equally appalled by what he saw as Barbauld's descent into the nursery: she 'was an instance of early cultivation, but in what did it terminate? In marrying a little Presbyterian parson, who keeps an infant boarding school, so that all her employment now is "To suckle fools, and chronicle small beer".'[18]

MARY ROBINSON AT DRURY LANE

From the time of her marriage to Thomas Robinson until 1800, when she retired to Surrey a few months before her death, Mary Robinson lived in some of London's most vivid and varied scenes. She was a regular visitor to Ranelagh and

Vauxhall, pleasure gardens contrived with complex and secret passages, in which strollers of different classes and desires mixed and flirted within an atmosphere of masquerade-like anonymity. She was also exposed to the more socially distinctive world of aristocratic gambling and libertinage to which her husband Thomas was drawn. But, though she moved in London high life, she knew the humiliation of having lived in the Fleet prison. She found her financial and intellectual salvation in the *demi-monde* nearby, combining lowlife and libertinage, art and squalor, in the artistic and theatrical world of Drury Lane.

Her social gaiety at this time suggests that, when Thomas Robinson was released from prison, Mary made up for lost time. I was not surprised to find that her recollections in her *Memoirs* devote much space to descriptions of the lavish gowns she wore, and lavish evening events she attended, juxtaposed with ongoing and practical efforts to produce domestic stability for her daughter, Maria Elizabeth. This paradox continues throughout Robinson's life: she is drawn to the life of pleasure and extravagance, dogged by her taste for expensive things and spendthrift men, while striving to be the central provider for her daughter.

The theatrical world offered a milieu in which she found glamour and intellectual stimulation as well as wages. Smallpox and then marriage having interrupted her earlier, she was now given an audience with Richard Brinsley Sheridan, successful author of *The Rivals*, who had recently bought a share of the Drury Lane theatre. Sheridan encouraged her, and Robinson prepared finally to make her debut, while Garrick, now retired from the stage, promised to give her guidance. During the first months of her life on the stage, Mary Robinson was pregnant, and she kept performing even while very close to term. In present day theatre and cinema, it is still unusual for an actress to appear while she is pregnant, and on television programmes pregnancy is either disguised or worked in as a feature of the plot. It is surprising and interesting that many eighteenth-century female performers worked while pregnant, and that there was a willing suspension of disbelief when a pregnant woman played a virginal heroine. However, Robinson's second daughter, Sophia, did not live more than six weeks after her birth in 1777 and Robinson spent the rest of that season recovering in Bath and Bristol. In her three seasons at Drury Lane (1777–80) she performed often and in good roles, including Ophelia in *Hamlet*, Octavia in Dryden's *All for Love*, and Cordelia in *King Lear*. She and Thomas were now living in the Piazza at Covent Garden, though her husband was thought to be keeping two mistresses.

Although we now approach Mary Robinson as a significant poet within a constellation of Romantic women poets, in her own lifetime she was known first as an actress and then as a Royal Mistress before finding her place and vocation in a literary milieu. Her affair with the Prince of Wales was enacted in public, another example of how her public life was constructed out of the vocabulary of private affections. And this again suggests both her self-consciousness and perhaps self-irony as well. Watching Robinson, now 22 years old, perform as Perdita in Garrick's altered version of Shakespeare's *A Winter's Tale* in early December 1779, the 17-year-old Prince fell in love with her, and had a series of amorous letters delivered to her through Lord Malden (later thought to be one of Robinson's lovers), signed with the name of the Shakespearean Perdita's lover, Florizel. Acting in a play turned into enacting the play in reality. The love between Florizel and Perdita was soon in all the London papers. The Prince and the actress played at being characters from a romance; they performed *as if* incognito before the urban audience. But, if Perdita in the play was born a royal, such final equality was not likely for Mary Robinson. Inevitably, Robinson's autonomy was bartered away in this love affair. It is likely that Robinson made the calculation clearly and understood the trade-off, by which she agreed, in 1780, to retire from the stage in exchange for financial protection from the Prince of Wales. When the Prince broke off the relationship a year later, Robinson claimed compensation from him, which her supporter Charles James Fox secured for her in 1783. Robinson wisely negotiated that her daughter would receive half of the promised £500 annuity after Robinson's own death.

A more humiliating price she paid was the series of satirical publications that coincided with and followed on from the affair, including the pornographic pseudo-*Memoirs of Perdita* as well as satirical poems and grotesque caricatures.[19] Though her relationship with the Prince lasted less than a year, Robinson continued, after her retirement from the stage and the end of the affair, to be represented in the press in caricature and squibs through public projections of her presumed private feelings. For example, at the Opera, the *Morning Herald* noted 'the pensive Perdita every now and then sent down an unavailing sigh' (17 Feb. 1780) when finding herself in a box near to the Prince and his new lover, Mrs Armistad.

Nonetheless, Robinson found herself welcome within the circle of power and influence around Charles James Fox, which opened avenues to financial security and both literary and political standing. As we would expect, her relations with Fox were rumoured to be sexual. In a 1782 letter to the Earl of Hertford, Horace Walpole quotes George Selwyn on Fox and Robinson: 'Who should the *man of the people* live with, but with the *woman of the people*?'[20] Walpole's obvious word play on different meanings of the 'public' woman as sex worker and the 'public' man as advocate of reform sets out strikingly the difficulty of the courtesan being taken seriously as reform intellectual or poet. Whatever she lost when her affair with the Prince had ended, through her intimacy with Fox Robinson underwent a political apprenticeship that strengthened her ideological links not only with Fox but also with the Duchess of Devonshire and with the forebears of what would become the liberal ascendancy of the nineteenth century. Fox and Sheridan were both committed to developing the Prince of Wales's autonomy from the King and his circle, and, with Robinson's potential for influencing the Prince, the three made an important, if transient, political partnership.

Not unlike that of Anna Barbauld, during these years Mary Robinson's work as a poet was an intermittent effort. *Captivity* was published in 1777, but it was the identity she developed as an actress that secured her a place in the metropolis through the mid-1780s. Robinson's intellectual and personal life had for some years been polished within the progressive Whig circle, and she worked hard to maintain her relations with those around the Duchess of Devonshire. In a letter to her brother John, written in 1784, Anna Barbauld includes Mary Robinson amongst the forward electioneering of the Duchess and her friends:

What do you think of the behaviour of our great ladies on the present election? I thought the newspapers had exaggerated: but Mr —— says he himself saw the two Lady ——'s and Miss ——'s go into a low alehouse to canvass, where they staid half an hour; and then, with the mob at their heels offering them a thousand indignities, proceeded to another. These he mentioned as unmarried ladies, and therefore less privileged. The Duchess of ——, Mrs ——, and many others, equally expose their charms for the good of the public.[21]

These women were not as morally exacting as Anna Barbauld, and one means by which Mary Robinson stayed in the hearts and minds of the Whigs was through visual representations. If she was not precisely well placed, her portraits certainly were, and they helped to erase the degradation of the various scurrilous satirical prints that arose from the affair with the Prince of Wales, which aim to ridicule him as much as her. The flurry of lovely paintings of Mary Robinson, in particular those by Gainsborough (1781), Romney (1781), and Reynolds (1782, 1784), suggest her 'natural' link to the titled families, and hint at a more lenient attitude towards sexual misdemeanours than that of the respectable middle class.[22] Quite unlike Anna Barbauld, who was considered beautiful by others, but did not call attention to her beauty herself, Mary Robinson did not stint in describing herself, her attractiveness to others, or her gorgeous clothing. But her beauty was central to her worth as an actress and sexual partner, and, as she had to sell herself (since her father did not take up the supervision of her sale in marriage, and her mother rather botched the job), the numbers of portraits from these years suggest Robinson's practicality. Portraits painted by important society painters raised her value, and, presumably wherever they hung, viewers would be interested in the history and connections of the beautiful sitter.

Eleanor Ty argues that Robinson had 'problems establishing and maintaining herself as a subject [i.e. a coherent subjective identity], partly because of public versions of her, as manifested in the cartoons, gossip, newspaper accounts, and artistic renditions'.[23] Ty distinguishes between an immature and a mature Robinson: the mature Robinson is close to Mary Wollstonecraft's model of feminism, and the immature

Robinson is exemplified by her capitulation to male stereo-
types, and her shifting and fragmenting sense of identities. I
am more persuaded by Judith Pascoe, who interprets Robinson's chameleonic capabilities as a method for getting round
and past the boundaries set up in front of her. The younger
and older Robinson had to be self-consistent in the structure of
her extraordinarily adaptive response to the vicissitudes of
daily life; her success in the world depended on it. The
spectacular differences in the ways she managed her life, from
tutor to actress to novelist, and the skill with which she
trumped her position as a gossip item to become a significant
literary editor attest to her skill at ducking and diving and
keeping herself afloat. Her actor's gift allowed her to mimic the
voices and personae that would supply her with financial and
social security.

Laetitia Mathilda Hawkins, a memoirist of the period,
catches exactly Robinson's ability to produce herself as an
imagined self: riding out in the social paths of Hyde Park,

> Today she was a *paysanne*, with her straw hat tied at the back of
> her head, Looking as if too new to what she passed, to know what
> she looked at. Yesterday she, perhaps, had been the dressed *belle*
> of Hyde Park, trimmed, powdered, patched, painted to the utmost
> power of rouge and white lead; to morrow, she would be cravatted
> Amazon of the riding house.[24]

In her 1799 *Letter to the Women of England, on the Injustice of
Mental Subordination*, Robinson writes, 'woman is denied the
first privilege of nature, the power of self-defence' (*LWE* 73).
But it may be the case that Robinson's most powerful self-
defence was her mimicry – not a conscious method of
subversion, but a talent for coping with the sorrows and
complexities of her life by taking the main chance. She was
preternaturally mature in her experiences of life – she learned
her brand of self-reliant feminism from the political and social
milieux that she threw herself into with such enthusiasm and
curiosity.

Robinson did not publish much poetry during her years on
the stage and with the Prince: her life was her art at that point,
though the lyrics she wrote for *The Lucky Escape*, a comic opera,
are clean and light and show her yet again able to mimic a

style with perfect results. But having lost one job as mistress, she found a new and more significant one: she fell in love with Banastre Tarleton, attractive veteran of the American Wars. When Robinson's daughter completed the manuscript of Robinson's *Memoirs*, she stressed Robinson's commitment to a relationship that 'subsisted during sixteen years' (*Per.* 131).

Tarleton returned to England as a Whig, and fell in with the same company as other oppositionists. His family was pressing him to make a suitable marriage alliance, and, though he may have been heroic in battle, he was a coward when it came to choosing a wife. Soon Robinson's personal life was again being performed on the stages of society gatherings and within the periodical press, the sixteen-year romance punctuated by semi-public separation and reconciliation. Unlike the relatively enclosed world of the Dissenting community in which Barbauld was situated, and which would only fully fill the public imagination during the revolutionary years of the early 1790s, Whig political life was inextricably yoked to personal and sexual intrigue. The power of women in exerting political influence is exemplified in the political life of the Duchess of Devonshire, who organized her dinners as the meeting place of the Foxites.

Robinson's desperate and manipulative poem of October 1788, 'Lines to Him Who Will Understand Them', which was published in the *World* newspaper, is a private poem written for the public. The lovers having fallen out, Robinson threatens to flee to Europe. The poem invites each stranger-reader to feel that they can identify a personal allusion that would be missed by another, less astute reader. The poem protects Robinson herself while beckoning to the public – allowing Robinson again to present the private in the public, and, in so doing, perhaps substitute the public gaze for the absence of true and intimate privacy. The poem's conclusion suggests that the move from Tarleton to solitude, and from England to Europe, will be the vehicle for Robinson's reanimation of her life as an intellectual – the poem is a declaration of poetic vocation:

> Torn from my country, friends, and you,
> The World lies open to my view;
> New objects shall my mind engage;

> I will explore th' HISTORIC page;
> Sweet POETRY shall soothe my soul;
> PHILOSOPHY each pang controul.
>
> (*SP* 89, ll. 53–8)

The tone of the poem also suggests that Mary Robinson is learning from Charlotte Smith as well as from Anna Barbauld. Now 30 years old, Robinson has had enough personal experience to find the model of the artless conversationalist no longer suitable to her poetic vocation. Much like Smith in her sonnets, Robinson acknowledges a personal defeat, and uses it to build a poetic of regret. Smith's poetry often rests upon her sadness as the essence of her being, without giving any details of her unhappiness. With Smith as her model, in this poem Robinson develops the landscape as a source of imagery and meaning. The empathetic relationship between the subjectivity of the poet and the objective world of nature belongs more to the world that will house Coleridge than to that of the abstracted pastoral figures of Robinson's earliest poetry.

In truth, however, the lived reality of public intrigue had become greatly diminished for Mary Robinson five years earlier, in 1783, when she was permanently disabled. In that year Tarleton was persuaded by his family to leave England for Europe, to escape financial problems – he was as badly in debt as Thomas Robinson. They were hoping, as well, that this would be the end of his relationship with Mary. His mother wrote to him sternly: 'It will give me real pleasure & satisfaction to hear that Your connection with Mrs Robinson is at an end; without that necessary step all my endeavours to save You from impending destruction will be ineffectual.'[25] Tarleton arranged to go to Europe, and, though Mary was pregnant with their child, offered to take her with him. Having refused, she then changed her mind, and paying off a portion of his debt, she set out after him, hoping to catch him up at Dover. On the way she experienced a bodily trauma that may have been a complication from a miscarriage, or a rheumatic fever – the evidence is not clear. Back in London the accident turned into an unmitigated disaster – Robinson never walked independently again.

The issue of Robinson's physical state was a continual undercurrent to her place in the public view. Her disability was always read as a symbol – of her pathos, her frailty, her decrepitude, or even her wickedness. A cruel letter from one aristocrat to another recorded that Robinson's 'face is still pretty, but illness has brought on a disadvantageous additional scowl to it; & as to her body she is quite defaite, *se trainant a piene*, a perfect Sciondolana'.[26] In 1794, four years after Robinson's death, William Gifford, the satirist and editor of the *Quarterly Review*, wrote a satirical poem, *The Baviad*, in which he maliciously urged his readers to: 'See Robinson forget her state and move / On crutches tow'rd the grave, to [the tune] "Light o' Love" . . .'. Another sentimental and cruel memoirist wrote of seeing the disabled Robinson at the Opera, 'not noticed, except by the eye of pity. . . . It was the then helpless paralytic Perdita.'[27] 'Mrs Robinson, or the Perdita, or the *Lame Sappho*', wrote another satirist, punning on the French *boiteuse* to describe badly made metre, and literalizing weak verse as physical lameness.[28] From 1783 until her death in 1800, Robinson's active literary life would be shadowed by ill health and the search for respite from her physical pains. A macabre error produced an obituary of Robinson in the *Morning Post* in 1786, when she was living abroad and taking cures at spas.[29] A week later, Robinson's letter was published, in which she claimed her life back, and also played down her injuries. 'I have the satisfaction of informing you, that so far from being *dead*, I am in the most perfect state of health; except for a trifling lameness, of which, by use of the baths at this place, I have every reason to hope, I shall recover in a month or six weeks.'

While her relationship with Tarleton would fitfully go on until his marriage in 1798 to Susan Priscilla Bertie, Robinson's professional life was now more firmly focused on the arts of writing rather than those of either beauty or acting. Laetitia Hawkins writes of this period that Mary Robinson 'then took up new life in London, became literary, brought up her daughter literary, and expressed without qualification her rage when her works were not urged forward beyond all others'.[30]

The 'new life' in London in the 1780s was socially and politically exciting, and would prove to be even more so after the events in Paris of 1789. Having had to set her acting life aside, Robinson revivified her life as a poet, and from 1788 onwards she rides the wave of popular poetry, one amongst the rising generation of women poets. Robinson's poems in this period work up the poetic of sensibility to a hyper-sensible pitch, and begin to include more overt paeans to the possibilities of political reform and liberty. In her 'Lines to Him Who Will Understand Them', Robinson also enters the space that will shift her poetic stance in line with the Della Cruscan poetics of Robert Merry and his predominantly female poetic correspondents. The London newspaper the *World* began publishing poems sent from Italy by a group of writers living abroad, headed by the liberal poet Robert Merry. Merry engaged in dramatized poetic relationships through the pages of the poetry columns of the *World* in 1787 and 1788. These public poetic exchanges offered the writers 'virtual' love affairs without the difficulties of acting them out. This redeployment of the rhetoric of intimacy in the most public venue – the newspaper – suggests a semi-articulated critique of the sociability metaphors of sensibility. Merry saw himself as a political liberal, and his poetry of excessive emotion was a counterpoint to conservative politeness. Mary Robinson apparently entered into this public poetic sequence by adopting the name 'Laura Maria', and she thus found herself a coveted contributor not only to the *World* but also to its successor, the *Oracle*.[31] Merry's original addressee in his poems had been Hester Piozzi, but he went on to address Hannah Cowley, who wrote under the name 'Anna Matilda'. I wonder if Robinson would have been pleased or annoyed to learn that, after her death, she was judged to have had 'a facility of composition almost approaching that of Mrs Cowley'.[32]

Robert Merry's poetry was considered by many to be ephemeral and overly ornate, and, though the distinguished critic Jerome McGann has aimed to recover the Della Cruscan poetic, it is difficult to explain or praise the mannered and cloying tangles of the Della Cruscan style. But the peculiar publicly private aura of the Della Cruscans was accessible to Mary Robinson, and it makes sense that she entered into the fray. The Della Cruscan form of publication was agreeable, but its style proved to be an unhelpful poetic model for Robinson's poetry. For example, her 'Ode to Della Crusca' overwhelms with its repetitive announcement of the sensitivity of the

'Patron of the sacred Lyre', as the speaker praises Merry's febrile verse as it

> Revibrates on the heart
> With magic thrilling touch,
> 'Till ev'ry nerve, with quiv'ring throb divine,
> In madd'ning tumults, owns thy wond'rous pow'r.

(SP 85, ll. 3–6)

But Robinson's public engagement with the group was useful to her as she again mimed an already formulated poetic to make her way through the literary world. Robinson was quite Keatsian as she rapidly took up and discarded poetic styles as she endured turbulent changes in her life.

4

Radical London: 1789–1791

The intellectual lives of Anna Barbauld and Mary Robinson flourished in the geography of radical London – a place not quite imaginary, but mapped by pamphlets, songs, and poems as well as by boroughs and streets, houses and taverns. Starting with John Wilkes's public campaigns for representation, and coming to include the organizations that corresponded with and celebrated the French Revolution, the rich urban culture of London in the 1780s and 1790s was built out of encounters between advocates of distinct religious, political, and cultural tendencies in a burgeoning urban print, tavern, and club culture and in the atmosphere of a new discourse of reform and democracy. Socially embedded distinctions between country and city, past and present, traditional society and the unmoored individual were half-broken, and produced an explosive and short-lived phenomenon, which brought artisans into contact with middle-class scholars, saloop sellers with intellectuals, rationalist revolutionaries with utopian collectivists, ballad-singers with ballad-collectors, aristocrats with Dissenters, and both Barbauld and Robinson with the ideology and culture of radicalism.

In 1787 Barbauld and Robinson had each recently returned from trips to Europe: Robinson settled in the Whiggish West End, and Barbauld and her husband in Dissenting Hampstead, an area implicated in the intellectual geography of London, but offering the comforts of village life. Anna Barbauld had been both attracted to and suspicious of the lure of the metropolitan life – in a letter to her brother she writes: 'I begin to be afraid we are got too much within [London's] attraction, for the nets seem to be winding round us; nay, we had some serious thought last week of setting up our tent here.' Rochement Barbauld was offered a place as minister to a congregation on what is now Hampstead's Rosslyn Hill, serving a community of like-minded middle-class Dissenters. The Barbaulds also had family and intellectual connections to the more activist Dissenting community around Stoke Newington, whose residents included Barbauld's sometime mentor Joseph Priestley, and Dr Richard Price, who preached at Newington Green and Hackney. In November 1789, Price delivered a sermon from the pulpit in the Meeting House of Old Jewry, making explicit a continuum between Dissenting and republican motives by arguing that the recent events in France were harbingers of a revolution that would replicate the Glorious Revolution of 1688. His sermon, and the meeting that followed it at the London Tavern, opened the debate about the meaning of the French Revolution that was codified in the argument between Edmund Burke's defence of traditional privilege, *Reflections on the Revolution in France* (1790), and Thomas Paine's argument for *The Rights of Man* (Part I, 1791). The Barbaulds were engaged in the most pressing contemporary issues upon their move to London, which occurred right around the time when a bill was before Parliament to repeal the discriminatory Corporation and Test acts.

After their travels abroad, Robinson and Tarleton returned to the West End, living in Clarges Street and later St James's Square. This was the town precinct of Whig society, housing the titled and near-titled, as well as clubs such as Brooks, which served as male enclaves to debate politics and gamble away money. The traditions of libertinage persisted amongst the radical aristocrats, which gave their interest in progressive causes the flavour of eighteenth-century radical chic. In Stoke Newington and Hackney and Hampstead, on the other hand, a strain of Dissenting severity dosed any overly enthusiastic revolutionary ardour. But, if the cultural geography of class kept Mrs Barbauld and Mrs Robinson on different sides of London, politically they were moving in parallel. The Dissenters of Stoke Newington and the Whig companions of Fox agreed on issues of religious toleration for Dissenters and Catholics, abolition of the slave trade, and, from 1789 until the September Massacres of 1792, the 1688 gloss on the French

Revolution – that is, constitutional monarchy.[1] And if Barbauld and Robinson as advocates of liberty did not meet at Whig literary salons or in the grand houses of St James's, they both dined at Joseph Johnson's literary soirées and, according to Horace Walpole, they both celebrated Tom Paine's rights of man in the imaginary geography of radical London. Meanwhile, across England, according to a contemporary newspaper, 'every Public house [had] copious libations . . . and "FOX AND LIBERTY" [was raised as] the universal toast'.[2] In this mood of cultural freedom, Anna Barbauld moved from the languages of Warringtonian amiability and devotional sensibility that had successively defined her work as daughter and teacher, into a new, *Romantic* language of political passion. The claims of *right* demanded ardour, not politeness. Anna Barbauld's Romanticism is not Jacobinism-in-recoil, but is tied directly to the clarion call of the French Revolution. Mary Robinson, for her part, found in the pursuit of the cause of 'Liberty' a cultural radicalism that distilled much of the sentimentality of her Della Cruscan poetry into a powerful social evocation of a better way of living.

ANNA BARBAULD IN RADICAL LONDON

Though we are used to thinking of later eighteenth-century London as a centre surrounded in the borough by self-enclosed villages, literary and political Hampstead residents such as Anna Barbauld and her friend the playwright Joanna Baillie felt themselves to be members both of the locality and of the metropolis. Access to town might often be made difficult by bad roads and weather, but there was ongoing traffic in and out of town, with a daily coach travelling between Hampstead and Oxford Street. By the later 1780s and 1790s, much of the Aikin family and the Warrington community had dispersed throughout the metropolitan area. While Rochemont and Anna Barbauld lived in Church Row, Joseph Priestley and Gilbert Wakefield were living in Hackney, and John Aikin moved to London in 1792, after being hounded out of Norfolk for his political positions. After a short time in Broad Street, he and his family moved permanently to Stoke Newington.

Certainly the print culture fostered through Joseph Johnson's press and social circle knitted together in print what
might appear disparate over space, and his supper parties
reinforced the connections between suburbs and centre. In
town, Joseph Johnson's building in St Paul's Churchyard,
which housed both publishing office and domestic quarters,
served his authors as an informal club. Right in the centre of
eighteenth-century London, the intelligentsia passed by and
through his shop. As his biographer points out, 'By publishing
with Johnson ... they enjoyed a kind of proximity to one
another that complemented their closeness in thought' as
liberal Dissenters.[3] By 1789, Johnson's authors were increasingly those associated with reform politics and a reformed
aesthetic as well. William Godwin and Henry Fuseli were
regulars, Thomas Holcroft, Wordsworth, and Blake were all
guests at one time or another, and the two great polemicists of
radical London – Price and Paine – took part in the long nights
of food and talk. Mary Wollstonecraft worked for Johnson in
the 1780s, being supplied by him with plenty of literary work,
and it was at his table that she found love as well as literary
interest in Fuseli, and, later, William Godwin.

Anna Barbauld, like Godwin and other London writers,
moved in more than one metropolitan social circle. She often
dined at the Portman Square house of Elizabeth Montagu,
where she observed 'the imposing union of literature and
fashion'; but it was while 'under the humbler roof of her friend
and publisher, Joseph Johnson', that she saw 'a chosen knot of
lettered equals'.[4] There is no doubt but that Johnson's circle
was lively, daring, artistic as well as politically radical, and
that it exerted a powerful influence on rationalist women such
as Wollstonecraft and Mary Hays.[5] For Barbauld, whose
experience and temperament had been shaped within a
domestic setting and with a set of domestic ideals, the evenings
at Johnson's might have been an adult and quite dangerous
version of what Warrington had offered years before. Barbauld's pedagogical practice of devotional sensibility changed
in her Johnson years. Amongst the explicitly radical Johnson
circle, politeness was less important than political passion. In
Johnson's dining room Fuseli hung his painting, *The Nightmare*,
so Johnson's dining club of discursive rationality was overseen

by the Romantic passions of that frightening and compelling dreamscape.[6] Barbauld turned her hand to the public issues of religious toleration, the slave trade, and the French Revolution, and made passionate claims for them in both poetry and prose.

She made a significant intervention into the pamphlet war around the proposed repeal of the Corporation and Test acts. Barbauld's *Address to the Opposers of the Repeal of the Corporation and Test Acts* was reprinted by Johnson twice in 1790. Her pamphlet explicitly linked the domestic political questions of religious toleration that had originated in the English Revolution of the 1640s with the international ones of 1789. Condemning the opposition to the repeal, she reminds her readers: 'England, who has held the torch [to illuminate France,] is mortified to see it blaze brighter in [France's] hands' (*SPP* 279). Johnson's pamphlet press offered anonymity – he published over fifty pamphlets on the issue of toleration – and this anonymity cut across the sexual division of intellectual labour that Barbauld had endorsed whilst at Warrington.[7] Dissenters such as Barbauld felt that events in France would help the domestic struggle for civic entitlement. The result was, however, quite the opposite: as Dissenters pressed their case, they were maligned in the press as threats to national security. Her polemic was printed within endpapers advertising other republican Dissenting pamphleteers, including the Warrington tutors Gilbert Wakefield and Joseph Priestley. Before the year was out, Barbauld's address had itself become the object of a set of 'strictures' by William Keate, rector of Laverton.[8] She was thus fully engaged in the public debate, as a 'citizen' rather than as an 'Authoress'. In her address, Barbauld articulates the enlightened rationality that aims for a universal constituency: 'We wish to bury every name of distinction in the common appellation of Citizen' (*SPP* 270). The pamphlet modulates from an ironic criticism of those who opposed the Repeal into a passionate advocacy of the French Revolution, drawing on the millenarian rhetoric associated with the spectrum of radicalism in the early 1790s:

> Can you not discern the signs of the times? The minds of men are in movement from the Borysthenes to the Atlantic. Agitated with new and strong emotions, they swell and heave beneath oppres-

sion, as the seas within the Polar Circle, when, at the approach of Spring, they grow impatient to burst their icy chains; when what, but an instant before, seemed so firm, spread for many a dreary league like a floor of solid marble, at once with a tremendous noise gives way, long fissures spread in every direction, and the air redounds with the clash of floating fragments, which every hour are broken from the mass. (*SPP* 277)

This address is grounded in a sense of intellectual entitlement, as Barbauld claims her right to speak of a 'certain, sure operation of increasing light and knowledge' (*SPP* 276). Against the implicitly moral manners of polite society, Barbauld insists 'Truth is of a very intolerant spirit. She will not make any compromise with Error' (*SPP* 269). She has brought with her from her Warrington education her focus on the universal and the rational, and from her Palgrave pedagogy the importance of language that is vibrant and emotional, but now her style is ignited by the excitement of current events.

In his 'strictures', William Keate groups together pamphlets by Priestley and Price and Barbauld as all belonging to a single persuasion and intellectual formation, and he singles out Barbauld's for its 'intemperance' and 'arrogance'; rebuking the author for not allowing 'himself time to cool' while admitting that the pamphlet's prose is 'animated'.[9] A postscript (which may be disingenuous) adds: 'since the above was at the press, the author hears, with infinite surprise, not unmixed with concern', that the pamphlet 'is from a female pen! "And in soft bosoms dwells such mighty rage?" '

In 1791 Johnson published under Barbauld's name her poem about the slave trade, the *Epistle to William Wilberforce, Esq. on the Rejection of the Bill for Abolishing the Slave Trade*. It was one of many abolitionist poems written by women throughout the debate, and quickly became an acceptable genre for women poets. Barbauld's description in the poem of the life of 'voluptuous ease' (*SPP* 124, l. 58) amongst the plantations may have been in part learned from the stories of the sons of planters who were educated and disciplined at the Warrington Academy. In the Warrington papers there is testimony that 'the West Indians were bewailing their native islands, and shocking the tutors by declaring that the earliest request of a planter's child was always for a "young nigger to kick" '.[10] Righteous indignation is the tone of the poem, and in it Barbauld makes an assault upon the corrupt rhetoric of current politics: she excoriates the 'flimsy sophistry'(*SPP* 123, l. 27) of parliamentary debate. With the publication of both her signed and anonymous pamphlets of 1790–3, which included her *Civic Sermons to the People* (1792) and *Sins of Government, Sins of the Nation* (a radical response to the idea of a Fast Day in April 1793 to purge the nation for its sins), Barbauld was fully engaged in the public arena of republican intervention.

Barbauld was now acknowledged as part of a circle defined politically, rather than familiarly. In 1790, with the storm raging in the Dissenting and Reform milieux about both the disaster of the defeat of the Repeal of the Corporation and Test acts and the marvelous explosion of the French Revolution, Walpole called her the 'Virago Barbauld'; and in 1791 she had become a 'poissoniere', a 'prophetess' ready to exercise her 'talons'.[11] And this passionate spirit was not only a public description; in her privately circulated poems of the period, Barbauld is proudly self-conscious of her shift. Her 'Lines to Samuel Rogers in Wales on the Eve of Bastille Day, 1791' links the urban and the revolutionary, and points away from the Warrington manner:

> Hanging woods and fairy streams,
> Inspirers of poetic dreams,
> Must not now the soul enthrall,
> While dungeons burst, and despots fall.

> (*PALB* 120, ll. 4–7)

Her charming and chiding letter adds: 'what have you to say in your defence for rambling amongst fairy streams & hanging woods instead of being at the "Crown and Anchor" as you and every good patriot ought to be on the 14th of July?'[12] That night was a significant one for the friends of the revolution in France, who were meeting to celebrate the Fall of the Bastille. A thousand people attended, and Robert Merry, Mary Robinson's Della Cruscan interlocutor, was there, contributing a song for the occasion.[13] Horace Walpole recorded that the event was broken into by government agents, and 'eleven disciples of Paine [taken into] custody': 'Mr Merry, Mrs Barbauld, and Miss Helen Maria Williams will probably have subjects for elegies.' The Warrington world, which aimed at 'rendering mankind not only mutually serviceable, but mutually agreeable', had given way to a world that was turning upside down, and in which to have a character 'in essence amiable' was no longer the desideratum: 'To please all the world . . . / Is no passion of mine', John Aikin wrote in his *Poems* of 1791, a certain mark of the change in habits of feeling associated with the new spirit of liberty.[14] Even the part of Barbauld's intellectual life least obviously touched by the events in France was stimulated and changed by the facts of the Revolution:

> The French Revolution will make all education altered, the ruin of classical learning. While other sciences, particularly that of politics and government, must rise in value, afford an immediate introduction to active life, and be necessary in some degree to everybody. All the kindred studies of the cloister must sink, and we shall rely no longer on the lean relics of antiquity.[15]

This impact was retrospective as well: the years between the Fall of the Bastille in 1789 and the execution of the French king in 1793 cast a new and more critical light on the past three decades. While Anna Barbauld was gathering rhetorical energy in the Johnson milieu, her fellow Warringtonian Gilbert Wakefield had also become increasingly radicalized. Wakefield held the Warrington image up to a somewhat tarnishing gaze in his *Memoirs* of 1792. In his acerbic reminiscences of the Academy, Wakefield looks back to the 1760s and 1770s with a demystifying eye, providing an irascible counterpart to the Aikin family narrative. Of John Aikin he writes that he could be very cruel to students, telling tales of 'mortifying instances of severity in the castigation of his pupils'.[16] Wakefield strips apart the apparently seamless links between polite conversation and rationality: of the Hebrew tutor at Warrington, John Taylor, he writes, he was 'very learned, liberal and rational', but as well 'peevish and angry' as a disputant, 'utterly impatient of contradiction, and dictatorial even to intolerance'. Wakefield argues that principle and friendship may often part company: he says that his pursuit of 'religious truth' could be undertaken only 'in opposition to the sensibilities of domestic influence' and 'the restraints of friendship'.[18] In the same year he published a pamphlet arguing against any kind of public worship, and Anna Barbauld published, again through Johnson's press, a set of 'strictures' against Wakefield's polemic. Her pamphlet shows her thoughtfully addressing the continuum of the domestic and the public: 'the sentiments of admiration, love, and joy, swell the bosom with emotions which seek for fellowship and communication. The flame may indeed be kindled by silent musing; but when kindled it must infallibly spread' (*RGW* 18). Barbauld's passionate argument for the civic goods brought about by public worship was the fruit of her own daily life. The urban radical Anna Barbauld was able to work as an autonomous intellectual principally through pathways of print culture and the quasi-public sociality of congregational worship. The democracy of public worship cuts across the hierarchy of gender distinction: 'Public Worship is a *civic* meeting. The temple is the only place where human beings, of every rank and sex and age, meet together for one common purpose' (*RGW* 43). While there is no evidence that she ever attended or raised a toast at radical celebrations in taverns, she could and did regularly attend the congregation.

Barbauld's periodical publications in the early 1790s included 'To a Great Nation, Written by a Lady' in Benjamin Flower's *Cambridge Intelligencer*. While the Johnson pamphlets rely upon anonymity to allow Barbauld to enter fully into the religio-political debate, the prominence given to the gender of the writer here seems quite pointed as a juxtaposition of polite and passionate rhetoric: perhaps there is a place, after all, for those 'dark unfriendly passions' she had shied away from when she was younger (*PALB* 2, l. 46). The poem suggests that a Lady can, without shame, write in the passionately analytical language of politics, rather than love: 'Nor virgin's plighted hand, nor sighs / Must now the ardent youth detain' from the dealing round of 'dreadful vengeance' (*SPP* 134, ll. 11–12, 2). 'To a Great Nation' is written in a song verse, quatrains of iambic tetrameter, like the large number of revolutionary songs written by radical plebeian clubs such as the Spenceans and poets such as Robert Merry, and sung in taverns and in partisan meetings supporting the French in their struggle against absolutism.

At this time, too, Barbauld wrote what later critics have found to be a perplexing poem, 'The Rights of Woman' (*SPP*

130), which appears to take a position firmly against Mary Wollstonecraft. In her 1792 *Vindication of the Rights of Woman* Wollstonecraft had criticized Barbauld's 'To a Lady, with some painted Flowers' (*SPP* 94), and William McCarthy and Elizabeth Craft argue that Barbauld's response is the work of a momentary irritation, rather than a programmatic argument about women's rights. It is certainly the case that Barbauld aims in this poem to elevate the universal case – exemplified in the identity of the 'citizen' – over any sexual division of labour or love, and she recoups the hierarchy of gender into a 'mutual love' that confounds the rationality of 'separate rights' (*SPP* 131, 1. 32). There is a hint of Barbauld's cultural naivety in this poem, and it is not surprising that she never intended it for publication. But the poem raises the question of what sort of relationship the two women had as two of the few female intimates of Johnson's circle. The degree to which Wollstonecraft and Barbauld were on amiable terms is not clear. Both Wollstonecraft and Barbauld were educationalists, and, using the Warrington tutor William Enfield's *The Speaker* as a model for her *Female Reader*, Wollstonecraft incorporated texts by Anna Barbauld into this anthology of readings for young women. Perhaps the best way to describe the difference between the two is as that between Dissenting and radical sensibilities.[19] Amongst the Aikin female historians, the anti-Wollstonecraft tendency became a family inheritance: 'The ladies of my family, though great admirers of Mrs [Mary Wollstonecraft] Godwin's writings, were too correct in their conduct to visit her, and the same objection was felt to Mrs Shelley.'[20] The different trajectories of the Aikins and the Wollstonecraft–Godwin–Shelleys mark out different lines in the politics of radicalism and republicanism in the late eighteenth and early nineteenth centuries. The Aikins' liberalism was rooted deeply in and bounded by their religious convictions; the Wollstonecraft–Godwin–Shelleys pressed their radicalism further until it fostered a version of political and aesthetic radicalism that adumbrates the democratic secular radicalism of the later nineteenth century. And we can see how antipathetic the close-knit Aikins would have found Godwin's public positions on domesticity: in 1793 Godwin had vigorously argued against the priority of familiar, in the sense of the familial, ties: 'My wife or mother may be profligate or a prostitute, malicious, lying or dishonest. If they be, of what consequence is it that they are mine?'[21]

In the ongoing dialectic of Anna Barbauld's works, the period of enthusiasm for the revolutionary impulse in France offered her the voice of a citizen, rather than a wife or sister. When the recoil came in the later 1790s and the Terror in France and the Terror put in place by Pitt had worked their destructions on revolutionary ardour, Barbauld returned to safer topics and to the narrower paths of the family and the Stoke Newington community of her brother John Aikin. The question remains of why Barbauld's poetic output was so slight in this period of her great intellectual enthusiasm, and why the poems she did publish or circulate are ephemeral or unsteady. My conjecture is that her usual poetic idiom was not plastic enough for what she wanted to write about now, and she was not able to redraw the boundaries of the poetic she had inherited, nor to adapt the poetic of amiable sociability to the ardour of the present moment. Her political radicalism was not accompanied by the same drive towards literary innovation or change, though she did master the pamphlet, the genre historically most suitable for polemic, and her *Civic Sermons* suggest her awareness of generic flexibility. Mary Robinson, on the other hand, though less confident of the principles underlying her support of political and social democratization, was able to reformulate her poetic to accommodate these new passions and concepts and thereby to help formulate the poetic genres of Romanticism and nineteenth-century sentimentalism.

MARY ROBINSON, CULTURAL RADICAL

Mary Robinson's years in radical London coincided with the successful public recognition of her poetic vocation. Looking back to the later 1780s in *Public Characters 1800–1801*, a compendium of short biographies and memoirs of contemporaries, the author of Robinson's obituary characterized the period as 'the age of female British authors', and names the poet as amongst those 'who have most eminently distinguished themselves amongst the numerous supporters of the female laurel'. With her gift for incarnating the *Zeitgeist*, Mary Robinson was now in the ranks of distinguished female writers. 'We congratulate herself and the public that her mind took this more satisfactory turn [towards literature]', the article continues, 'because it afforded not only an improved use of time, but has been the cause of engaging her attention to general delight'.[22] This comment suggests a new moral as well as vocational turn in Robinson's life and in her social milieu. By the end of the century, the Hyde Park-charioteering Perdita had become the sentimental heroine of her own *Memoirs*, and, through her achievements in the new poetic of simplicity, she became a poetic intimate of Wordsworth and Coleridge. Robinson's transition from Royal mistress to Friend of the People to philanthropic poet was catalysed by her place within John Bell's publishing enterprise. Bell was a friend of both Sheridan and Fox, and the publisher of the Della Cruscan poet, Robert Merry. In 1787, when Bell and Edward Topham issued the *World* as a newspaper venture with both sporting and literary features, it was a quick success, selling 3,000 copies of Number 1, which included in it a tribute to 'Laura Maria's [Robinson's Della Cruscan pen-name] beautiful sonnet'. Bell's links to the Whigs and Topham's to the theatre through his relationship with the actress Mary Wells – a frequent contributor to the paper – may have made their publication receptive to Robinson's work. Bell was the principal publisher of the Della Cruscans, which linked him with the erotic liberalism of Merry and his poetic correspondents. In 1789 Bell broke with Topham, and on 1 June he issued a new paper, the *Oracle*, bringing his literary contacts downmarket with him and developing a tarnished reputation for his radicalism: in 1794 he faced down charges that he was too liberal, and he asks his readers whether in twenty years of publishing they have detected in him 'any *seditious* tenets? Any *Gallic* Blasphemy? Or any symptom of Jacobinism?' (*Oracle*, 24 June 1794). Starting out as the friend of Fox and the Prince of Wales, Bell ended bankrupt, and when his case came before magistrates, he asked that the adjudicator be the loyal Joseph Johnson.[23]

Mary Robinson's most sustained period of writing poetry coincided with the period of revolutionary and reform radicalism; and her most significant poem in the first years of the

French Revolution is *Ainsi va le monde*, published first by Bell in 1790 as a single volume, with a portrait by Joshua Reynolds. The publication announced Robinson's entry into the exciting yet principled world of the liberal intelligentsia. Robinson was in the company of many who were sympathetic to the French Revolution, for the new radical morality permeated both the gambling and the chattering classes. Robinson's sometime patron, the Duchess of Devonshire, was also drawn to the sociality of the reform network, and her long friendship with Charles James Fox gave her prominence in the periodicals and print press. Though Robinson no longer moved extensively within the social world of Whigs, she and they alike began to gravitate towards circles of middle-class intellectuals who were shaping the political thought that would motivate the next century in Britain. But there were difficulties for Robinson. Though Anna Barbauld and her brother and community were as one, for example, in support of Wilberforce's Abolition Bill in Parliament, it is likely that Mary Robinson's position set her apart from her lover Tarleton, who, as a Parliamentary Representative for Liverpool, was not in favour of an end to the slave trade. Not uncharacteristically, Robinson found a way to balance her emotional dependence and vocational autonomy.

Ainsi va le monde provides a map to Robinson's changing preoccupations; in it she draws together her public and confidential personae through the Della Cruscan mode, and by the end of the poem she offers a manifesto for freedom that Thomas Paine might admire. When Robert Merry urged the link between sensation and liberty, writing the 'Laurel of Liberty' in praise of the events in France, Robinson immediately responded with *Ainsi va le monde*, reputed to have been written in twelve hours. The note in her *Memoirs* (probably added by her daughter) that describes this outburst of impassioned writing figures Robinson as the embodiment of poetic spontaneity rather than measured decorum. Though Robinson continues her habit of exhibiting the intimate as the public, her poetic persona in *Ainsi va le monde* is very different from the one she had presented in her *Poems* of 1775. Here she offers an *ars poetica* that links the poetical and the political. Without any apparent sense of the contradiction within her extravagant praise of Merry, Robinson argues that at present poetry has become too 'fantastic' and the poet must 'pluck the weeds of vitiated taste' (*SP* 105, ll. 54, 58). She argues that reform of poetry and reform of politics are mutually dependent. Rather than drawing on her catalogue of classical motifs, Robinson now invokes a Rousseauvian 'Nature' rather than 'Fancy' (*SP* 106, l. 68). Not long afterwards, Coleridge bridged the gap in poetic theory between nature and fancy by discriminating between Imagination and Fancy, the former being a quasi-natural function that belongs to all persons, the latter a method of producing images. As in her poems in the 1775 volume, Robinson values the rural above the urban, but now her natural world is an animating one, infusing persons with the natural desire for Heaven's 'noblest attributes': 'Ambition, valour, eloquence' (*SP* 108, ll. 165–6). And, although Robinson invokes a new start for poetry, she offers it as the outcome of a history of poetic Genius, naming Milton, Shakespeare, Chatterton, Otway, and now Robert Merry (and, by implication, Mary Robinson herself). She steers a course between the idiosyncratic and the imitative by arguing that the poet must position herself within the tradition, for 'emulation kindles fancy's fire', yet to merit true praise 'the voice of kindred genius must be true' (*SP* 107, ll. 119, 130). When she invokes the pure spirit of Freedom she writes: 'What gives to Freedom its supreme delight? / 'Tis Emulation, Instinct, Nature, Right' (*SP* 112, ll. 283–4). Qualities of intellect and of material life together compose the conditions of a free people and a free poetry.

This introduces the theme that will reappear at the end of the poem: an appeal to 'Freedom' that Wollstonecraft noted in her review of the poem, and that Robinson's daughter, Maria Elizabeth, removed from the 1806 edition – evidence of the reaction against reform during the long years of the Napoleonic Wars. Robinson argues that, through the medium of freedom, reason opens out both political and poetic capacities: 'From her, expanding reason learns to climb . . . She wakes the raptures of the Poet's song' (*SP* 109, ll. 168, 170). What is then explicitly politicized in the following verse paragraphs is a brief history of despotism in France, presented first as the abstract principles whereby Nature, Freedom, and Genius are all integrated.

As she moves on to her poetic history of oppression in France, Robinson articulates her allegiances both home and abroad. She describes how in France 'the rights of man' have been given over to 'rav'nous power'(*SP* 111, l. 255), using the Enlightenment reform phrase that would become identified with Paine's 1791 tract, with its republican implications: 'Who shall the nat'ral Rights of Man deride, / When Freedom spreads her fost'ring banners wide?' (*SP* 112, l. 292). And she uses a term that will become popular in Britain in the reform movement of the 1830s and 1840, 'social love' – those 'rapt'rous energies' (*SP* 111, l. 256) and feelings of comradeship with others – which also owes to the cult of sensibility the yoking of sympathy and political justice.[24]

The final section of *Ainsi va le monde* is spoken by a poetic persona who could not be mistaken for the polite poetess of the 1775 volume. Robinson puts into play Della Cruscan erotic conventions with radical politics: she asserts the links amongst reason, eloquence, the rights of man, and a notion of a social whole within which the category of emulation will become redundant (interestingly, she does not use the term again in the final rising movement of the poem). Robinson's training in sensibility meets up with the political urge towards freedom in a set of highly wrought feminine metaphors: 'Freedom' appears 'In dimpled smiles and radiant beauties drest' and 'Cherubs' throng round her as hairdressers who 'prepare / Enamel'd wreaths to bind thy flowing hair' (*SP* 113, ll. 325–6).

By the end of the poem Robert Merry is lost to view. In his place, the spirit of Freedom and the poetic speaker fuse as the cry of ' "Freedom" echoes thro' the vaulted skies. / The Goddess speaks!' (*SP* 114, ll. 339–40). Mary Robinson becomes the Goddess, the newcomer to the poetic tradition she has earlier outlined. In *Ainsi va le monde* Robinson writes confidently, ready to make judgements about others as well as recognizing her own worth. She had travelled quite a distance from the evocation of oppression in *Captivity*: some of this, no doubt, derived from her increased confidence as an adult who had dealt with a series of scandals and misfortunes, and some from the growing influence and publicity of women intellectuals. In the atmosphere of metropolitan radicalism, bluestockings and radical feminists – Barbaulds and Wollstonecrafts – were not only coming into conversation with each other, but also offering models for self-made women like Robinson. As she organized her place within poetic tradition, Robinson forged an association with the name of Sappho; Judith Pascoe, noting its frequent use in discussion of Robinson, suggests that she might in fact have given herself that name, and then answered to it.[25] The *Oracle* defined her talent as breathing, 'The tender Strain of SAPPHO with the soft pathetic Melancholy of Collins' (29 July 1789). In *Public Characters of 1800*, the author vindicates the Sapphic claim: 'We have seen Mrs. Robinson censured for taking the signature of "Sappho". It would have been *wise* if her censors had remembered, that it was they themselves (the reviewers) who first assigned to her that title.'

As she enters into the volatile and exciting world of 1790s literary and political culture, Mary Robinson presents herself as a poetic genius – a Sappho, a political reformer – calling for 'rights of man', while not relinquishing her role as complex lover, whose subjectivity is the stuff of a romantic heroine. Her sonnet sequence of 1796 *Sappho and Phaon* was an important part of her self-representation as a tempest-tost abandoned lover. In *The Poetics of Sensibility*, the distinguished critic Jerome McGann makes the case that this sequence belongs to a genre of mid-1790s coded poems, in which political issues are presented through elaborate metaphorical strategies that would have been understood by fellow radicals but not by the prying eyes of a by now rabid campaign by the state against democratic goals. I remain unconvinced by this argument, however; Robinson's unflagging desire to exhibit herself to best advantage seems to me to be demonstrated in the *Sappho and Phaon* sequence. She identifies herself with a Sappho of great beauty, passionate (heterosexual) feelings, and poetic genius, abandoned by a Tareltonesque lover. As a personal vindication and a public reputation-builder, *Sappho and Phaon* accomplishes a major task for Robinson: to my mind, the sonnet sequence's politics are neither apparent nor decipherable, and its poetic ornaments drown its passionate narrative.

But, in 1791, *Ainsi va le monde* reached a large and politicized audience when it was republished in Robinson's well-received volume of *Poems* (expanded into a two-volume edition in 1793). Much of the 1791 collection comprises Robinson's Della

Cruscan interchanges with Merry, poems steeped in the imagery of Italian vistas and imbued with the contemporary sense of Italy as a place of experiment and beauty. There are many scantily disguised allusions to her affair with Banastre Tarleton in a series of poems of love and betrayal. Her status as a disabled woman also makes her evocation of retirement shift from metaphoric to literal meaning; in 'The Adieu to Love' she writes of a retreat from amorous battles:

> In still Retirement's sober bow'r
> I'll rest secure; – no fev'rish pain
> Shall dart its hot-shafts thro' my brain.

$$(SP\ 94,\ ll.\ 16–18)$$

Her lines to Tarleton, only partially disguised as 'Lines to Him Who Will Understand Them', adumbrate the tone and persona of Byron's heroes: she will abandon England, as Childe Harold will later do, and

> breathe the spicy gale;
> Plunge the clear stream, new health exhale;
> O'er my pale cheek diffuse the rose,
> And drink OBLIVION to my woes.

$$(SP\ 90,\ ll.\ 81–4)$$

It is notable as well that a great number of the poems in this volume are odes, securing their contemporary and sentimental content to one of the most capacious classical genres.

Robinson's *Poems* of 1791 ends with a democratic theme in *Ainsi va le monde*, but the work is materially rooted in high-society Whig circles. At a moment when subscription publishing was giving way to market publishing, the patron list for Robinson's 1791 *Poems* is a *Who's Who* of London social and literary circles. Subscribers included not only the Prince of Wales as well as his brothers the Dukes of Clarence and Gloucester, and most of Tarleton's family, but also Fox and the Duchess of Devonshire; among the many literary, academic, and artistic subscribers were Mrs Mitford, De Loutherberg, Reynolds, and a number of Cambridge Fellows. When the *Critical Review* reviewed the volume in 1791, it noted that the work 'exhibits a numerous list of subscribers from the first rank of title and fashion'. Reynolds's frontispiece portrait of Mary Robinson shows, not an actress in role, but the figure of the poet of sensibility, looking out over an oceanic emptiness. The volume proves to a public that Robinson has triumphed over failed love affairs and physical disability. She followed up this poetic visiting card by establishing a salon where she would receive those 'men of distinguished talents and character' in whose houses she might not be welcome.[26] There is less comment in the 1790s on Robinson's difficulty in walking, and more on her persistent 'nervous illness', which was tacitly understood to be an effect of Tarleton's treatment of her from 1788, when she is described as returning from France 'deeply affected and oppressed in spirits' (*Morning Post*, 31 Jan. 1788) through the late 1790s, when readers of the newspapers are alerted that 'Mrs Robinson has been confined to her bed these last ten days with a nervous fever' (*Oracle*, 5 Feb. 1798). Mrs Robinson was no longer a sex goddess, but a neurasthenic, liable to public sympathy.

In fact, Robinson began to experience numerous falls linked to her rheumatic condition in the 1790s, which made it very difficult for her to write, and harder for her to manoeuvre around on crutches. In 1793 she fell and injured herself. While she lived in London, she was mobile in her carriage, and there is a bitter continuum from the overdecorated carriage that she rode in when mistress of the Prince of Wales, with its pseudo-royal insignia, to the necessary conveyance when she could no longer walk. A most poignant moment arrived in 1797, when Robinson, still living in London and heavily in debt, was forced to sell her carriage.

The second edition of Robinson's *Poems* (1793) appeared as two volumes, and to it Robinson added various topical poems. Many English reformers had reconsidered their supportive position towards the events in France between the constitutional monarchy established in 1791 and the execution of the King in 1793. It had been the events of 1789–91 that Wordsworth, amongst others, saw as a parallel to England's Glorious Revolution of 1688, France's 'forerunners in a glorious course'. But this identification threatened, after the regicide, to uncover the memory debris of the English regicide of 1649, which had lain for over 100 years beneath the apparently benign Glorious

Revolution of 1688. Charles James Fox had been an important supporter of the 1789 Revolution, and he felt that the defeat of the absolutist government meant France might no longer be considered the chief enemy of England.[27]

Anna Barbauld and Mary Robinson also changed their attitudes and ideas in relation to the changing events in France in 1791 and 1793. Robinson deepened her sense of what liberty might offer, but within a narrower compass – compassion and empathy – and she was drawn again to her interest in the social world of the aristocracy. Barbauld found that the assimilation of Dissenting to establishment families was now cut short by the public association of Dissent with Francophilia. Both poets were basically Foxites, though Robinson's was foremost a personal connection that then lead to a political connection. Fox himself was well liked by Dissenters: he was entirely devoid of religious impulse and engaged in no practice, so he could hardly feel offended by the Deists amongst the Dissenters, and his Enlightenment motives made him work on behalf of Dissenting enfranchisement.

With the King executed and the Queen in captivity, and war between France and Austria underway, English supporters of the moderate sort were falling away. Because Fox believed in the French Revolution as first and best a re-enactment of 1688, he was shocked by the turn of events. Not in favour of the despotism of Louis XVI, he nonetheless did not favour ending the French monarchy altogether. In the period after the execution of the King, Fox balanced arguments against royal despotism against those that sympathized with the plight of Marie-Antoinette. Edmund Burke's depiction of the terror experienced by Marie-Antoinette opened up a rich vein for sentimental identification, which Mary Robinson was able to develop in her poems on the Queen.

Although the outward shape of Robinson's life seems drawn in relation to her love affairs, she took great interest in and modelled herself on a series of women who appeared to have either secure or patrician lives. I have already touched on her desire to situate herself and her poetic vocation through a tradition of women poets, from Sappho to Smith. But models in the world she lived in were also precious to her. She admired the actress Mrs Jordan, but it was Georgiana, Duchess of Devonshire, who offered the image of the beautiful and wild, but absolutely well-positioned woman of public and private life. Even in her 1799 *Letter to the Women of England, on the Injustice of Mental Subordination*, Robinson's arguments (many of which are similar to those put forward in Mary Wollstonecraft's *Vindication of the Rights of Woman*) against women's oppression are posed in the language of and by reference to the customs of the aristocracy of both birth and genius. For Robinson, as for Edmund Burke, Marie-Antoinette offered the image of a beautiful, faithful, martyred woman. First printed in the *Oracle* under her Della Cruscan pseudonym 'Laura Maria', 'Marie-Antoinette's Lamentation' imagines the inner voice and sensibility of the doomed queen. The link between feeling and writing is presented on the queen's breast as she offers 'A dreadful record – WRITTEN WITH MY TEARS' (*SP* 135, l. 6). The Queen's being is presented entirely through her maternal role as she weeps for her children: the poem folds back the public role of Queen into the private one of mother, 'Oh! All the MOTHER RUSHES TO MY HEART' (*SP* 137, l. 66). There is a strikingly different tone to this poem from the companion text Robinson wrote about the royal family, 'Fragment. Supposed to be written near the Temple, at Paris, on the night before the Execution of Louis XVI' (*SP* 127). The King's fragment is written in the fluent eighteenth-century style of personification, inflected by Miltonic gravity and Gothic intensity. Robinson here focuses on the position of King, and on the political emotions of ambition, malice, suspicion, and anarchy. The third of Robinson's royal poems is her 'Monody to the Memory of Marie-Antoinette', which was published in the *Oracle* on 18 December 1793. This poem develops at length the female and maternal issue; the 'dark demons of destructive ire' have trampled upon the 'domestic virtues, glitt'ring round the Throne'. Brutally ejected from the world of private emotion, 'maternal woes' are turned inside out and become 'the rabble's jest' (*PWMR*, i. 58, l. 58). Robinson identifies with the way in which sorrow and terror have transformed Marie-Antoinette's personal beauty:

> Mark, in her alter'd and distracted mien,
> The fatal ensigns of the pangs within!

> See those fair tresses on her shoulders flow
> In silv'ry waves, that mock the ALPINE snow!
>
> (*PWMR* i. 61, ll. 146–9)

Robinson appears to have identified with the maligned Queen: 'Shunned be the MONSTER, who, with recreant art, / Beyond the GRAVE, would hurl Detraction's DART!' (*PWMR* i. 63, ll. 283–4). The Monody is written in the high public style, its similes made of grand comparisons: the King as eagle, the Queen as the sun itself. By calling the poem a Monody, Robinson puts her work in the tradition of Milton's *Lycidas*. It is a fitting genre as well for the English Sappho, as the monody is a genre distinguished as the voice of a single speaker (as opposed to a choric work) – in this speech Robinson binds her own identity closely to that of Marie-Antoinette. The classical monody was thought to have been sung to a private audience, as at a symposium. This appears to be another instance of Robinson making public records of what are linked as well to private feelings, and of course the content of the poem is that of private domestic virtues being punished on the public stage of the guillotine. She reverts as well here to drawing on the poetry of pastoral retreat rather than urban clamour: 'Now to his REAP-HOOK, and his pastoral reed / The crimson'd PIKE and glitt'ring SWORD succeed' (*PWMR* i. 72, ll. 512–13). Robinson calls for the 1688 sense of Liberty, which would not 'require / The CHILD should perish for the guilty SIRE', nor 'inspire the ATHEIST'S breast, / To mock his God, and make his LAWS A JEST' (*PWMR* i. 74, ll. 573–5).

In the continuation of Robinson's *Memoirs*, her daughter records an intimate erotic moment between Mary Robinson and the Queen taking place during a public event. This happened shortly after the birth of the Dauphin at the time of Robinson's visit to Paris in 1781. Invited to a grand supper, only

> A small space divided the Queen from Mrs. Robinson, whom the constant observation and loudly whispered encomiums of Her Majesty most oppressively flattered. She appeared to survey, with peculiar attention, a miniature of the Prince of Wales, which Mrs Robinson wore on her bosom, and of which, on the ensuing day, she commissioned the Duke of Orleans to request the loan.

Perceiving Mrs Robinson gaze with admiration on her white and polished arms, as she drew on her gloves, the Queen again uncovered them, and leaned for a few moments on her hand. The Duke, on returning the picture, gave to the fair owner a purse, netted by the hand of Antoinette, and which she had commissioned him to present, from her, to *la belle Anglaise.* (*Per.* 123)

Without speaking to one another, Robinson and the Queen gaze intensely at each other, the Queen focused on Robinson's bosom, and Robinson on the Queen's 'white and polished arms'. Robinson appears to be as irresistible to the French as to English royalty, and the Queen takes advantage of her attention by seductively responding to Robinson by drawing her gloves on and then off again. Soon the Queen is sending a gift and a note, much as 'Florizel' did a few years before. Sentimental heroines, Marie-Antoinette and Mary Robinson both bring intimacy onto the political stage, eroticizing their troubled lives and offering them to a rapt audience.

One of the most interesting poems in the 1793 volume is 'The Maniac', a poem that adumbrates the linked discourses of poetic composition, drug-induced reverie, automatic writing, and madness that takes off in Romanticism and continues through the occult edge of modernism, later reproduced as a methodology in psychoanalysis and surrealism. 'The Maniac', according to Robinson's *Memoirs*, was dictated aloud after she had taken eighty drops of laudanum, dictated so rapidly that it could not be written down as fast as it emerged. The next morning Robinson 'was perfectly unconscious of having been awake while she composed the poem' (*Per.* 138) – a very early anecdote of what the surrealists called 'automatic writing'. This is, of course, an anecdote that might well have inspired Coleridge's preface when he published 'Kubla Khan' in 1817.

'The Maniac' also suggests the problem of subjectivity that permeates Robinson's best volume, *Lyrical Tales*. The empathetic heart of the speaker reaches out with comfort and pity to the 'dismal moan' and 'agonising shriek' of '*mad Jemmy*' (*Per.* 138). But there is a major block between the inarticulate cries of Jemmy and the sympathy extended by the speaker, for her urge towards understanding the maniac is met by the conundrum of his opacity:

Oh! let me all thy sorrows know;
With THINE my mingling tear shall flow,
And I will share thy pangs, and make thy griefs my own.

(*SP* 124, ll. 52–4)

Jemmy's inability to speak his sorrow provides the impenetrable barrier between them. The speaker watches the inhuman reciprocity between the maniac and the natural world as he 'howl[s], responsive to the waves below' (*SP* 123, l. 21). As she struggles to make sense of the horror of his distraught mind, his inarticulacy increases her own anxiety: his gaze appears to her as the horror of flat affect.

Ah! quickly turn thy eyes away,
They fill my soul with dire dismay!
For dead and dark they seem, and almost chill'd to STONE!

(*SP* 124, ll. 46–8)

The poem proceeds as a series of increasingly desperate questions as the speaker projects all *her* terrors onto *his* template of madness. The poem ends as a stand-off, the speaker still imploring but unable to enter into correspondence with the maniac. She ends reiterating her desire to 'ENCHANT THEE TO REPOSE', but we feel that she has lost her own repose. The narrative of her automatic composition of the poem adds to our sense that the poet herself, for these hours, has lost her own identity in her pursuit of understanding his. The voice of this poem is stripped of excess ornamentation, and suggests the path that Robinson will follow in her *Lyrical Tales*, where she is able to marshal the simplicity of balladic style to guide and make safe the presentation of the subjectivity of the outcast, the lonely, and the mad.

Having cast Mary Robinson as a Zeitgeist chancer, I now want to add that her voice in these poems is rather more 'authentic' than I might have supposed. Pretending to a sociable circle of stable polite families was certainly an exercise in fantasy; and the amorous encounters with Della Crusca were evidently good for Robinson's developing a career as an 'English Sappho'. But, given the ongoing and mostly unsuccessful struggles she engaged in to keep her family out of poverty, and to shape an identity for herself, it makes sense that the attraction to the new language of rights would be stimulating and productive. *Ainsi va le monde* is one example of this. Nonetheless, those of Robinson's poems that treat of the contemporary political world follow a course laid down, on the one hand, by the opinions and influence of Fox, and, on the other, by the founts of sensibility that linked genteel life to affective sensitivity. When Fox was effectively marginalized by his positions on the French Revolution, Robinson began pulling up her stakes and moved on. In the future, her politics would find its way forward through the subjective politics of democratized poetic form in her use of the ballad, and a more generalized post-Della Cruscan sentimental poetics in her poems that formed the posthumously published *The Progress of Liberty*. It might be right to say that Robinson became a Romantic poet through a combination of the same political alterations as moved both Wordsworth and Coleridge, and the personal poetic relations developing amongst all three during her time as poet/editor of the *Morning Post* in the last three years of her life. The later 1790s see Robinson turn further away from *demi-mondaine* values on the fringes of Whig aristocracy, and towards the morality of a liberal middle class.

5

Barbauld and Robinson amongst the Romantics

In 1794 the energetic domestic reformers and radicals went to ground. 'Jacobins-in-recoil', as E. P. Thompson called the generation of Romantic poets who converted the fire of righteous indignation into the mellowness of meditation, emerged at the end of the century with a new version of how poetry might change the world. The period after the French regicide was a confusing time for activists and intellectuals: their silence and self-scrutiny registered the general shock at the acts of repression introduced by the British state, acts that were fuelled by the memory of the English regicide. Over the next few years the alliance of high and low radicalism collapsed and the urban community bound together by optimistic liberalism dispersed. Joseph Priestley left for America, and the American model of liberty began to enter more fully into the reform and Dissenting consciousness – the symbolic ground of not only Southey's and Coleridge's dreams of a Pantisocracy, but also Anna Barbauld's important ruin poem, *Eighteen Hundred and Eleven*. After 1794, the dismay amongst the Dissenters who saw their bid for full entitlement swamped by association with French radicalism was matched by confusion amongst the metropolitan Whigs, and, while many remained committed to the principles of liberty, they worked to disengage its discourse from the immediate French context.

LIVING VOCATIONS AND PROFESSIONS

As Anna Barbauld and Mary Robinson adjusted to the atmosphere of sobriety in the later 1790s, and retreated from the publicity of London radicalism, each took on new and serious tasks within the publishing and newspaper worlds. Robinson began her association with the poetry page of the *Morning Post*, the newspaper of the Whig opposition throughout the 1790s, which culminated in her position as the newspaper's chief poet. Barbauld wrote steadily for the series of Dissenting journals associated with her family: the *Monthly Repository*, John Aikin's *Monthly Magazine* and *Athenaeum*, and later her nephew Arthur's *Annual Review*. Robinson took on the role of poetry arbiter for the *Morning Post*, offering a public forum for the new poetry of Wordsworth and Coleridge. Anna Barbauld was a canon-shaper, editing texts for the reading public, including Akenside's *Pleasures of the Imagination*, an edition of Collins's poetry with a prefatory essay, and, in the first decade of the nineteenth century, the extraordinary set of prefaces to a fifty-volume edition of the *British Novelists*. Robinson's editorial decisions created a public for avant-garde poetry; Anna Barbauld codified the literature of the past. Their influence as literary authorities was defined in this period; their status was grounded in their earlier literary achievements. Personal crises may have urged them on as well. By 1798 Banastre Tarleton had broken entirely with Mary Robinson; and Rochemont Barbauld had become mentally ill, abusing and threatening his wife. He committed suicide in 1808.

Barbauld and Robinson emerged from the early 1790s with greater confidence in their personal power and their talents, and the desire to engage with new literary manners and talents. As Stuart Curran points out, Mary Robinson was quick to associate herself with the style she found in Southey's poetry, and soon after in work by Coleridge and Wordsworth.[1] Although Anna Barbauld's own writing voice did not change significantly, her model of conversational poetry might well have influenced Coleridge, and she, like other poets, returned to and developed the resources of meditative and domestic verse during the war years. It is worth considering the encounters amongst Robinson, Barbauld, and Samuel Taylor

Coleridge to assess how Robinson and Barbauld made sense of the contemporary reconfiguration of poetic conventions and cultural norms: the move from metropolitan to rural Romanticism. While Mary Robinson threw herself into the new poetry of simplicity, with hardly a backward glance at her days as an ornamented Della Cruscan – her cultural radicalism hurrying her into the future – Anna Barbauld struggled to find forms and forums for conveying her Enlightenment values and devotional sensibility.

MARY ROBINSON, SATIRIST AND ROMANTIC

In 1794, the year in which the government unsuccessfully attempted to make examples of four radicals by trying them for treason, and a range of legislation was enacted that compromised the rights to free assembly and speech, Robinson produced her social farce, *Nobody*, which was performed a few times to the great outrage of titled ladies who were the object of her satire. Her earlier cultivation of aristocratic Whig Grande Dames was now modified by her growing confidence and skill as a social critic. As might be expected, *Nobody* was interpreted as the work of an upstart. The play makes fun of women gamblers, attacking a putative vice of upper-class women. The Drury Lane prompter William Powell wrote in his diary that, at the play's first performance, the noise 'from the Opposition of Hisses and Applauses, [was so loud that] not scarcely three lines of that could be distinctly heard'. Even as Robinson gravitated to the norms of respectability that were overtaking those of sensibility, she maintained her worldly-wise assessment of the high life. One of the qualities that made her a popular poet in the *Morning Post* was her skill at writing satirical and topical poems. This style of Whig urbanity allowed Robinson also to cast an ironic glance at her own foibles – writing versified and epigrammatic squibs that satirize fashionable styles and habits. These poems are not tied to her sentimental feminine pseudonyms, and are articulated in a voice that is satirical while also comic in the largest sense: life affirming and celebratory. Most striking are those that actively acknowledge and celebrate London as the source of personal freedom and autonomous identity. 'London's Summer Morning', 'January 1795', and 'The Poet's Garret' are fine examples of this sub-genre. Judith Pascoe notes that the first of these poems owes much to Swift's 'Description of the Morning'. Written in August 1800, a few months before Robinson's death, the poem honours the variety of urban sights and sounds:

> Now begins
> The din of hackney-coaches, wagons, carts;
> While tinmen's shops, and noisy trunk-makers,
> Knife-grinders, coopers, squeaking cork-cutters,
> Fruit-barrows, and the hunger-giving cries
> Of vegetable venders, fill the air.
>
> (*SP* 352-3, ll. 9–14)

The survey is shaped by the sounds, not the sights, of the street, yet each noise, particular and distinct, conjures an image and becomes part of the soundscape. The poem ends wittily as the 'poor poet', lying in bed and listening to these sounds now 'wakes from busy dreams, to paint the summer morning' (*SP* 353, ll. 41–2) in words that she has seen through sound.

'January 1795' gives a comic portrait of the competing personae of London life:

> Poets, Painters, and Musicians;
> Lawyers, Doctors, Politicians;
> Pamphlets, Newspapers, and Odes
> Seeking Fame, by diff'rent roads.
>
> (*SP* 357, ll. 29–32)

This poem has a direct source in a 1738 poem by John Bancks, who presents the same elements but with a far grimmer and cynical tone:

> Lawyers, poets, priests, physicians,
> Noble, simple, all conditions:
> Worth beneath a threadbare cover,
> Villainy bedaubed all over.[2]

It may be that the author of this poem was the same Bancks who was a London bookbinder and bookseller, and who had come to the metropolis after an apprenticeship in weaving in

Berkshire. Like Mary Robinson herself, he had been disabled early in his life. And, like Robinson's, his was a fairly insecure and aspirational life. He wrote a biography of Oliver Cromwell that he signed as a 'Gentleman of the Middle Temple', though no one has found evidence for his gentility, but the energy of city life is evident in his poem. Robinson held onto the trochaic reversal for a pair of satires on contemporary fashion, both printed in the *Morning Post* in 1799, 'Modern Male Fashions' (*SP* 360) and 'Modern Female Fashions' (*SP* 362). Having left the world of Hyde Park fashionable drives herself, she appears to be confident enough to let her own previous sartorial silliness be an object of satire:

> Cravats, like towels thick and broad,
> Long tippets made of bear skin:
> Muffs, that a RUSSIAN might applaud,
> And *rouge* to tint a fair skin.

(SP 362, ll. 9–12)

One of her last poems, 'The Poet's Garret', makes kindly fun of the figure of the city poet, living in romantic squalor: 'At the scanty fire / A chop turns round, by packthread strongly held' (*SP* 354, ll. 28–9) and surrounded by unfinished texts:

> Here a page
> Of flights poetic – there a dedication –
> A list of dramatis personae, bold,
> Of heroes yet unborn.

(SP 355, ll. 56–9)

In 1794 and 1795 Robinson, though still involved with Banastre Tarleton, was receiving less from him than she gave. When she earned money for her novels, she gave it to Tarleton, who then spent it in gambling. But fearing betrayal and shut out of the fashionable world by illness and reputation, Robinson became more interested in and attracted to elements of the intellectual world who came from the middle class rather than the aristocracy, and whose values were domestic and moral. Robinson became an intellectual hostess. James Boaden, editor of the *Oracle* during Robinson's public years, recalled going to her house in 1794, where she invited visitors and 'delighted in the opportunity it gave her of hearing all that passed in the world, and of mingling in the conversation her full share of intelligence and grace – she still *sat* a remarkably interesting woman, and disdained to intrude upon conversation any evidence of pain actually suffered at the moment'. Boaden reported that *Nobody* and Mary Robinson's 1797 novel, *Walsingham*, 'have done much to overturn Faro [a popular gambling game] and his Host. If report may be credited, no one has more reason to execrate a gaming table than this lady.' The *Oracle*, always a supporter of Robinson, helped in its squibs to build the version of Robinson's identity that is fulfilled in her *Memoirs*: a wronged and fragile woman, defrauded by gambling scallywags, and struggling for authenticity. Boaden saw her paralysis as the outward sign of an inward penitence that has 'severely expiated the errors of her early life'. During the last years of her life, Boaden asserted, 'The respect of the liberal part of society she always retained'.[3]

The masks of 'Tabitha Bramble' and 'Portia' allowed Robinson to write cultural criticism without Della Cruscan ornament or sentimentality. At the same time, she continued to elaborate her self-presentation as the living 'Sappho'. I mentioned earlier that the *Sappho and Phaon* sequence has been read as a coded discourse of radicalism. Though Mary Robinson is often strategic and manipulative in her work, she is hardly ever coded, except in places where the code is meant to be easily cracked, as in the later novels and the poems to Tarleton. Robert Bass more convincingly argues that the sonnet sequence is a dramatization of the turbulence of Robinson's relationship with Tarleton, which is later turned inside-out in her vengeance poem, published just a few months before her death. In 'To a False Friend. In Imitation of Sappho', the divine afflatus becomes an avenging whirlwind, pursuing the beloved and his new love: 'In vain you fly me! on the madd'ning main / Sappho shall haunt thee 'mid the whirlwind's roar' (*PWMR* iii. 199, ll. 19–20). When Tarleton finally succumbed to his family's wishes and married Susan Priscilla Bertie, Robinson took her revenge in two novels she published in 1799, *The False Friend* and *The Natural Daughter*. These were *romans-à-clef* designed to portray both Tarleton and his wife as villains, and they make bookends for Robinson's self-vindication in her *Memoirs*.

In addition to these contrasting poetic registers of social satire and inward sentimentality, in the *Progress of Liberty* Robinson worked in a voice that married abstract theory to the new valuation of rural life as the site of natural democracy. This set of poems, published together in 1806, offers stylized versions of Liberty and Anarchy, and culminates in the domestic liberty of the rural harvest,

> Where Earth presents her golden treasuries;
> Where balmy breathings whisper to the heart
> Delights unspeakable!

(SP 320, ll. 67–9)

Most important, however, were the poems that used a less elaborate language of sympathy and self-scrutiny – poems published together in 1800 as *Lyrical Tales*.

Robinson the romantic heroine and Robinson the Romantic poet were both irresistible to Coleridge. Both poets were associated with the *Morning Post*: theirs was a short, intense, poetic, and personal connection, though its intimacy was what we might think of as a 'virtual' one – taking place through the media of letters, poems, and publications. They met for the first time in January 1800, introduced by Godwin, who had recently met and been impressed by Robinson's beauty and intelligence. Daniel Stuart, the editor of the *Morning Post*, had installed Robinson as main poet contributor after Robert Southey had left for Portugal at the end of 1799.[4] Between them Southey and Robinson contributed hundreds of poems to the paper, and Stuart watched the daily circulation rise from 350 in 1793 to 3,500 by 1803.[5] Coleridge was signed on as a staff writer in 1799 to write political articles. It is tempting to think of the affinity between Robinson and Coleridge as grounded in their particular relation to, in Coleridge's case, plagiarism, and, in Robinson's, mimicry. Both poets were drawn to the forms and subjects conceived by others, and for both it was a way of establishing a sense of identity to compensate for personal insecurity and the feelings of being an outsider in the world. Coleridge was far less nimble and self-aware, and his reputation suffered throughout the nineteenth and twentieth centuries from claims being made of his using others' ideas, even their words, without citation, passing them off as his own.[6]

Robinson, as an actress, was more conscious of how an actress must be both herself and the other body she is filling in for – and she brought this talent with her into her poetry of the 1790s. Nonetheless, her *Lyrical Tales* are often considered as imitations of Wordsworth and Coleridge's *Lyrical Ballads*. Yet it was Wordsworth who acknowledged his debt to Robinson for the metre of 'The Solitude of Binnorie', a poem that she published in the *Morning Post* on 14 October 1800: 'Sir. It would be unpardonable in the author of the following lines, if he omitted to acknowledge that the metre (with the exception of the burthen) is borrowed from "The Haunted Beach" of MRS ROBINSON, a most exquisite Poem.' In fact, it is unlikely that Robinson herself knew that it was Wordsworth who wrote both the lines and the acknowledgement, since Coleridge appears to have sent the work to her as his own![7]

Robinson had described the composition of her 1791 poem 'The Maniac' as induced by a dose of opium, and Coleridge echoed Robinson's acknowledgement of her opium-induced poem-making in his own preface to 'Kubla Khan', a preface published seventeen years after Robinson's death. When she read the poem in manuscript in 1800, Robinson responded by using 'Kubla Khan' to underwrite her own poetic variations upon his theme in 'To the Poet Coleridge':

> Now by the source which lab'ring heaves
>   The mystic fountain, bubbling, panting,
> While Gossamer its net-work weaves,
>   Adown the blue lawn, slanting!
> I'll mark thy *sunny dome*, and view
> Thy Caves of Ice, thy fields of dew.

(SP 330, ll. 9–14)

Robinson is a straightforward borrower here. On the practice of opium taking itself, as with poetry, Robinson writes with candour; Coleridge with guilt. As Martin Levy points out, Mary Robinson used opiates intensively in her final illness, and she refers openly to it in poems printed in the *Morning Post* in 1800. Robinson acknowledges the pleasures and pains of opium, 'From the POPPY I have ta'en / Mortal's BALM and mortal's BANE' (*PWMR* iii. 315, ll. 65–6), while Coleridge throws a veil of regret and ambivalence over his allusions to his struggle with opium. Perhaps Coleridge admired Robinson's unvexed relation to issues that for him were terribly fraught. Though Robinson's enthusiastic opportunism makes her temperamentally very unlike the shame-ridden Coleridge, it is easy to see why the easily allured Coleridge was drawn to and identified with her. Plagiarism is a dirty secret, while mimicry is a public talent. And where Coleridge alternately laments and aims to cover up his faults and misdemeanours, Robinson can take an amused pride in her own: 'I'm odd, eccentric, fond of ease; / Impatient; difficult to please' (*SP* 141, ll. 55–6).

As a practising hypochondriac, Coleridge took an interest in Robinson's illness, and he persuaded his friend the scientist Humphrey Davy to prescribe something for her rheumatic pains. Not surprisingly, Coleridge quickly began to complain of his own rheumatism. Coleridge's comment about Robinson is touchingly suggestive of how he would be described by others: 'She overloads every thing; but I never knew a human Being with so *full* a mind – bad, good, & indifferent, I grant you, but full, overflowing.'[8]

Robinson continued her public connection with Coleridge by writing an ode to his son, Derwent. Here Robinson uses her Sapphic mask, her 'sad heart sighing o'er her feeble lyre' (*SP* 327, l. 98); but, in her self-imaging as a 'stranger' singing to Derwent from 'lone her forest haunts among / The haunts of wild-wood harmony' (*SP* 327, l. 93), she brings together ornamented sentimentality with the type of the Romantic solitary – the ubiquitous rural wanderer of Wordsworth's poetry.

Although she never relinquished her links to London, and her work for the *Morning Post* kept her at the centre of urban discussion, in the last six years of her life Mary Robinson spent increasing amounts of time in Old Windsor, where she had gone first with the Prince of Wales, and where she later spent solitary periods in retreat. After Tarleton's marriage in 1798, Robinson installed herself and her daughter, Maria Elizabeth, at Englefield Cottage. Robinson's attachment to her daughter was always strong, and at Englefield Cottage her daughter became her lifeline. When Robinson died in late 1800, her daughter took on the task of publicly presenting her mother, completing Robinson's *Memoirs* in the voice of the sentimental apologist. It was at Englefield that Robinson assembled the lyrical ballads she had published in the *Morning Post* into her most impressive achievement, *Lyrical Tales*.

Robinson was, as usual, able to judge the mood of the moment, making a voice for the culture of the single, rather than the social, self. She was now the best model of the new 'spirit of the age' – writing poems that were both lyrical and democratic, giving voices to the dispossessed and the displaced. Robinson was quite straightforward about the link between her work and Wordsworth's: the volume, she wrote to a prospective publisher, would be 'in the manner of Wordsworth's Lyrical Ballads' (*SP* 54).

Rather than using a London press, she sent the work to Wordsworth and Coleridge's Bristol publisher, Joseph Cottle. Although she was a good bet for any publisher, in choosing to publish with Cottle, Robinson was publicly identifying herself with the coterie of poets of the new movement. Dorothy Wordsworth complained in a letter that Mary Robinson had pinched the title, so that William considered altering his title for the second edition of *Lyrical Ballads*: 'Mrs Robinson has claimed the title and is about publishing a volume of *Lyrical Tales*. This is a great objection to the former title [*Lyrical Ballads*].'[9] Robinson was also reclaiming her Bristol nativity – the returning prodigal daughter. But Wordsworth also benefited from Robinson's interest in his work. The established poet Robinson had offered a place to the neophyte poet by choosing Wordsworth's 'The Mad Mother' for the *Morning Post*. And, while Robinson was looking to Cottle to place her within the orbit of the Bristol circle, Wordsworth was seeking urban attention, asking Cottle to sell the copyright for *Lyrical Ballads* to Joseph Johnson, whose imprint Wordsworth wished to be associated with, for its tradition of liberal politics and its links to the centre of the London intelligentsia.[10]

The problem of influence, derivation, and poetic Zeitgeist is a difficult one to resolve. In 1954 Robert Mayo published an article, 'The Contemporaneity of *Lyrical Ballads*', in which he shocked his audience of literary critics by showing how *Lyrical Ballads* was not an entirely new kind of poetry, but a somewhat better version of a popular fashion in recuperating the ballad tradition. In fact, Coleridge, Wordsworth, Robinson, and Southey were all mining the same interest in lyricism within narrative, and simplicity in style. They were all drawn, as well, to the powerful and often contradictory combination of an enchanted countryside with its cooperative practices and superstition, juxtaposed to the desperate living conditions caused by bad harvests, war, and the pressure of extreme poverty. The four poets were in a continuous practical conversation with one another on the poetry page of the *Morning Post.* Less overtly than the Della Cruscans, the first public generation of Romantic poets made the new poetry as a collective, if unselfconscious, coterie. Though not often considered as one of the group, Mary Robinson was as active and important as Southey, Wordsworth, and Coleridge in creating the genre of Romantic balladry.

So what are the distinctions of value to be made between Robinson's *Lyrical Tales* and Wordsworth's *Lyrical Ballads?* Robinson's metrical advantage is clear; and, as Stuart Curran has pointed out, her interest and skill in the technology of metre were an important source for the later Romantic poets Felicia Hemans, Letitia Landon, and Elizabeth Barrett.[11] As an innovator in the lyric, Robinson used the thematic possibilities of the ballad as magical, mysterious, simple, plebeian, and rural to build a bridge between her narrators and their subjects. Her tales endow both narrator and subject with equal claims to subjective entitlement, the cultural counterpart to the claims for civic entitlement that shaped the reform movement through the nineteenth century. While Wordsworth's ballads emphasize distance from their objects of scrutiny, by focusing either on the character of the narrator himself (as in 'We are Seven') or on the pathos of the person described ('Simon Lee' or 'The Female Vagrant'), Robinson's give access to the protagonist's interior life, and present that life as an interiority not different in kind from the narrator's. If Wordsworth wanted to be a man speaking *to* men about other men and women, Robinson writes ballads in which her narrator speaks as one *amongst* other men and women, and whose speaking breaks down the distances between them. In her ballads, interiority is not the exclusive property of the narrator/poet, as it can be in Wordsworth, often chillingly as in 'Old Man Travelling', where the human subject is reduced to rocklike insentience. Yet, while Robinson's ballads assert and aim for full connection between the human subjects and objects, they also come up against the isolation of interiority, and how the material experiences of poverty and displacement throw us deep into ourselves, often in a deranging way. So the promise of the democratization of interiority – the claim in the ballads for the selfhood of the displaced, the fugitive, the foreign, and the poor – must struggle with the gravitational pull of the black hole of selfhood.

Readers of Robinson's 'All Alone' will see it as a corrective of Wordsworth's 'We Are Seven'. In 'All Alone', the sympathetic narrator not only understands the isolation of an orphan weeping by its mother's grave, but tries to break through it with her assertions of understanding. It may not be the case that we are satisfied that the connection is made – the child cannot emerge clearly enough from its self-involvement, but the poem makes the identity of speaker and subject its poignant theme. Wordsworth's 'We are Seven', quite differently, uses the example of a rural child's intuitive understanding of the community of the living and the dead to admonish the narrator, by making a comic presentation of the narrator's psychological obtuseness, but the end result is the erasure of the child in favour of this ironic presentation of the narrator.

In 'The Lascar', Robinson writes a domestic oriental tale, in which the landscape of England is transformed into something utterly unlike itself through the subjectivity of a refugee. Though he 'sigh'd to greet this fertile soil', a displaced East Indian youth is now starving and harassed, and 'fev'rish pain, / Maddens the famish'd LASCAR's brain' (*SP* 198, ll. 60–1). In a leap of identification, the narrator gives us the boy's experience of geographical confusion as he wanders in a landscape that he makes his own, which makes us see the familiar as if different.

> Again the Summer Sun flam'd high
>   The plains were golden, fair and wide;
> .   .   .   .   .   .
> The insect myriads humm'd their tune
> To greet the coming hour of noon,
> While the poor LASCAR BOY, in haste,
> Flew, frantic, o'er the sultry waste.
>
> (*SP* 200, ll. 97–8, 105–8)

When the youth, shut out from English hospitality, has starved to death, the Englishness of the scenery returns:

> And now the village throngs are seen,
>   Each lane is peopled, and the glen
> From ev'ry op'ning path-way green,
>   Sends forth the busy hum of men.

(SP 200, ll. 301–4)

What appears to be a green and pleasant land to some is felt as a desert by the displaced and the foreign. The poem is a brilliant commentary on imaginative insularity.

'The Fugitive', linked thematically to Robinson's other poems about French exiles and victims, bears some comparison with Wordsworth's ongoing cast of vagrants and discharged soldiers. Wordsworth's 'Old Man Travelling', like the 'Discharged Soldier' fragment and 'The Female Vagrant', quickly become admonitory symbols – whose purpose is to guide the narrator into his poetic vocation. In 'The Fugitive' the object of Robinson's scrutiny becomes a speaking subject through her voice, and changes her in the exchange. He 'loiters, sad and mute' (*SP* 215, l. 10), not because of an intrinsic mystery about him, but because he cannot speak English. A priest in flight from France, the fugitive cannot speak, but his visible sign – the tear that rolls down his cheek – communicates directly with the narrator:

> Poor Traveller! Oh tell me, tell me all –
> For I, like thee, am but a Fugitive
> An alien from delight, in this dark scene!

(SP 216, ll. 34–6)

The lyric 'I' opens out to the human object and reanimates him by translating him. While Wordsworth's Old Man, like his later Leech-gatherer, has turned into unconscious nature, Robinson's 'Fugitive' is resuscitated through the breath of the poem's 'I'.

In the *Lyrical Tales*, Robinson's gift of mimicry is transubstantiated into identification and animation. Of all the pathways that Robinson moved through in order to become herself, this one seems to be the most authentic. Surely this comes in part from her own experience of being a lifelong domestic alien: not quite in the polite society to which she, like her father, aspired, nor yet resigned to the slipshod life offered by her debt-ridden and philandering husband. Mary Robinson was able to make important poetry out of the radical politics she had learned from London intellectuals, by marrying her knowledge of the conventions of sensibility to the subjective realities experienced by the alienated, isolated, deracinated wanderers of her age.

The active writing network of Southey and Robinson and Wordsworth and Coleridge suggests that not only was Robinson a Romantic poet in the sense that she wrote within the age of Romanticism, but that she was a fellow, not a follower, of the central Romantic poets. Nonetheless, what we poignantly experience reading *Lyrical Ballads* and *Lyrical Tales* after 200 years is that, while Wordsworth's volume inaugurated his poetic vocation in the world of print culture, Robinson's gives us a hint how suited she was to write and develop in a more democratized poetic milieu. The *Lyrical Tales* are the least masked and most confident of her poems. Robinson described her ballads as 'my favourite offspring' – most adored, because latest and least expected. Sadly, they were her last poems.

ANNA BARBAULD IN STOKE NEWINGTON

Anna Barbauld had a more complex relationship with the young Romantic poets, not least because she lived well into the nineteenth-century and she was increasingly treated as a remnant from another age. In 1800, the year Mary Robinson died, Anna Barbauld was 57 years old.

Like other Dissenting radicals and rationalists in the mid-decade recoil from the French Revolution, Barbauld meditated on her earlier poetic and polemical interventions, and produced a series of domestic and personal poems that are moving not only for their precise evocation of the value of the everyday, but also for their retrospective, elegiac tone. Her 1795 'Autumnal Thought' offers a poignant retrospect of her period of political passion. This autumn takes place after the 'fervid Passions' of radicalism have been tranquillized

> And Judgement, late, begins to rule;
> When Reason mounts her throne serene,
> And social friendship gilds the scene.
>
> (*PALB* 130, ll. 15–17)

But for that loss of passion, she cannot find Wordsworth's 'abundant recompense'; at the very moment of equanimity, she realizes the cost of quiet: 'But O, the swiftly shortening day! / Low in the west the sinking ray!' (*PALB* 130, ll. 9–10). The balance of loss and gain is hard to maintain, and her intimation of the afterlife, when 'The flames that drank our vital strength' are 'assuaged at length' (*PALB* 130, ll. 1–2), recognizes the declension of 'failing spirits [that] prompt no more' (*PALB* 130, l. 25).

'Washing Day' may have been written before the 1790s, but it was first published in the *Monthly Magazine* in 1797, and it suggests how Barbauld's public presentation emphasized that her world was shrinking to the proportions of the private sociability of family. But now the private is conceived more particularly in terms of personal inwardness. Though the mock-heroic elevation of the events of domesticity is typical of eighteenth-century satire, 'Washing Day' modulates into a personal poem, made up of anecdote that stresses the child's experience of the domestic ritual:

> I well remember, when a child, the awe
> This day struck into me; for then the maids,
> I scarce knew why, looked cross and drove me from them;
> Nor soft caress could I obtain, nor hope
> Usual indulgences.
>
> (*SPP* 146, ll. 58–62)

There is a lovely picture here of Anna Aikin, the child reasoner, as she would 'sit me down, and ponder much / Why washings were' (*SPP* 146, ll. 78–9).

As Rochemont became mentally unstable, Anna relied more and more on her brother, and in 1802 the Barbaulds moved to Stoke Newington to be near John, who had moved there in ill health in 1798. There the family became involved in local activities – Rochemont held the ministry at the Newington Green chapel, while Anna founded the local book society – and distanced itself from national issues.[12] The move to Stoke

Newington was a return to the more intimate social circle of the Warrington period. John Aikin set the tone of this period of practical social activity, and he steered the family away from radical politics.

Many of the radical Dissenters had been broken by the radical years. The Aikins' great friend and publisher, Joseph Johnson, was tried and imprisoned for publishing Gilbert Wakefield's excoriation of the Bishop of Llandaff.[13] Wakefield, long an interlocutor and friend of the Aikin family, also spent a year in prison and died soon after in 1801. Just after his release, John Aikin wrote a poem to him in the temper of defeated Jacobinism, in which he invited Wakefield to 'Cease then, my Friend, thy generous hopeless aim', put aside his politics and return to a more amiable muse:

> Take serene
> The tranquil blessings that thy lot affords,
> And in the soothing voice of friendship drown
> The groans and shouts, and triumphs of the world.

The passionate radical and internationalist aim of 'fraternité' has turned into a more local and familiar idea of friendship. Wakefield replied in a poem, also published in Aikin's *Monthly Magazine*, in which he refused to take that route, vowing still to 'Front the grim visage of despotic power, / Lawless, self-will'd, fierce, merciless, corrupt'. He died before the next year was over.[14] The following year John Aikin declared: 'I am cured of all theoretical ideas of reform.'[15]

In this atmosphere of political retrenchment, Barbauld began a new phase of her intellectual life, codifying a tradition of literary value, and reinforcing the ethical codes she had believed in all her life. Barbauld developed her role of literary arbiter, using her power as an editor to produce editions of Collins' poems, a collection of essays from the *Spectator* and *Tatler*, and Richardson's *Letters*. Her great contribution to formulating both a tradition and contemporary taste was her edition of the *British Novelists*, for which she wrote long prefaces, and which she accomplished in less than two years, the full set completed in 1810.

In 1797 Barbauld met Coleridge and began her brief connection with him. She and Coleridge also had a poetic

correspondence, and she wrote an admonitory poem 'To Mr.
S. T. Coleridge', counselling him to pay more attention to his
duty and activity, and to watch out for indolence, a catchword
of criticism from the Enlightenment Dissenting community
and probably a bit galling to Coleridge:

> Youth belov'd
> Of Science – of the Muse belov'd, not here,
> Not in the maze of metaphysic lore
> Build thou thy place of resting; lightly tread
> The dangerous ground, on noble aims intent.

(SPP 143, ll. 32–6)

He in turned was first amazed by her and her brain, and then
sceptical of what her values entailed for his generation of
poets. When he met her for the first time in 1797, he described
'that wonderful *Propriety* of Mind! – She has great *acuteness*,
very great – yet how steadily she keeps it within the bounds
of practical Reason.' But Barbauld was a literary judge from the
older generation, and, though their politics coincided for a
period, her rectitude was probably not very comforting to
Coleridge. An anecdote that exemplifies this generation gap is
part of Coleridge's *Table Talk*: seven years after Barbauld's
death Coleridge recalled that she had complained that the
'Ancient Mariner' had no moral, and he had replied that in fact
it had too much moral! Coleridge also publicly maligned her
in a lecture in 1813, after her reputation had already suffered
through attacks on *Eighteen Hundred and Eleven*. The character
of the attacks became increasingly vulgar and cruel. Crabb
Robinson, a long-time friend of Mrs Barbauld, said that
Coleridge had made a joke about Rochemont, who 'must have
had a very warm constitution, he had clasped an icicle in his
arms for forty years before he found it was cold'.[17] Charles
Lamb, Coleridge's dear friend, joined in, complaining that
Barbauld's children's stories were designed to dampen the
imagination. These complaints tell us that, in the early nineteenth century, Barbauld's influence was pervasive enough to
be an easy target for the new generation of poets.

Nonetheless, Barbauld's impact on the Romantics was for-
mative. There is a connection amongst Robinson, Barbauld,
Wordsworth, and Romantic ballad poetry through the work of

William Taylor, a Dissenting minister from Norwich, with whom Barbauld was close, and whose translations of the German poet Bürger were critical to the ballad revival of the end of the century.[18] Barbauld had educated Taylor at Palgrave: he called her 'the mother of my mind'. Taylor published his translations of and essay on Bürger in the *Monthly Magazine*, which Southey read and to which he contributed. Taylor's essay predicts the discourse of Wordsworth's preface to *Lyrical Ballads*: '[Bürger's] extraordinary powers of language are founded on a rejection of the conventional phraseology of regular poetry, in favour of popular forms of expression, caught by the listening artist from the voice of agitated nature.'[19] In 1794 Barbauld recited Bürger's *Lenore* to a party in Edinburgh, and it was afterwards recited to Scott, who later wrote that this experience had spurred him to write ballad poems himself.[20]

In 1826, the year after Anna Barbauld's death, a short elegiac poem she had written on 'Life' (1812) was praised by Wordsworth as having a last stanza that he wished *he* had written:

> Life! We've been long together,
> Through pleasant and through cloudy weather;
> 'Tis hard to part when friends are dear;
> Perhaps 'twill cost a sigh, a tear;
> Then steal away, give little warning,
> Choose thine own time;
> Say not Good night, but in some brighter clime
> Bid me Good morning.

(SPP 126, ll. 23–30)

It is easy to see the appeal of this poem: written by a very old poet, it sentimentalizes the approach of death as the end of a friendship with life. It returns to the tone of Barbauld's *Poems* of 1773 – familiar and polite – but speaks to the reader schooled in sentiment as well as sensibility.

In 1808 Rochemont Barbauld became violent and tried to murder Anna with a kitchen knife. She escaped and soon afterwards the two separated. It was a dreadful experience for her to find her partner of so many years deranged into her enemy: in a letter to a friend she describes how 'I feel wounded in the tenderest part, a part for which I had provided no armour'. In November he drowned himself in the New River, and Barbauld became severely depressed: 'Day after day passes, and I do not know what to do with my time; my mind has no energy, nor power of application.'[21] Yet she did work very hard in the two years after Rochemont's death, writing the prefaces to the fifty-volume edition of *The British Novelists*, published in 1810. An essay in which Barbauld produced some of the first sustained writing about the novel as a literary form and one with its own history accompanied the edition of twenty-eight novels written by twenty-one novelists.

During Rochemont's illness, the family gathered to support Anna. John Aikin and his son Charles (who had been raised by the Barbaulds when they first moved to Palgrave) kept a close eye on the crisis, and made the arrangements for the separation. But, invincible, Anna Barbauld was soon writing out of a renewed strain of independence and analytical passion. In the year after the publication of *The British Novelists*, she wrote *Eighteen Hundred and Eleven*, her strongest intellectual piece, a poem that displays a poetic maturity perhaps glimpsed but certainly not achieved in her Warrington poems.[22] More fully independent than she had ever been – without father or husband – Barbauld speaks with a voice that is authoritative and severe, and that works a brilliant change on the ruins-of-empire motif. The poem was written during the war between England and France that had been going on for almost twenty years. Although reformers and radicals had opposed the war when it began in 1793 as a direct response to the French Revolution, by 1811 the atmosphere was one of fatigue and despondency, brought about by the emotional, physical, and economic sufferings of war, and a great degree of patriotic cohesion.

I began this study with a discussion of *Eighteen Hundred and Eleven*, and readers might want to go back to that now, having learned more about Barbauld's intellectual history. Here I want to point out that one of the most impressive aspects of the poem is her presentation of London, the site of her emancipation into intellectual discourse and personal autonomy. Writing more than a decade after she had first moved to London, Barbauld projects the city into the future, buffeted by time and the course of empire into a ruin. She first presents the ideal of

London that was hers when she arrived in the late 1780s. This is a city startlingly unlike that Warrington ideal of the balance of freedom and regularity; instead, London's boundaries are 'irregularly great' (*SPP* 167, l. 161). The metropolis is a great cauldron of diversity and possibility, with 'No jealous draw-bridge, and no closing gate' (*SPP* 167, l. 162). Unlike many of Barbauld's early 'conversation' poems, intimately addressed to a friend or relative (a style Coleridge brilliantly adopted), this is a very public poem, whose interlocutor is Britain the 'island Queen' (*SPP* 162, l. 40). But if its elevated stance marks one difference from Barbauld's early poems, it nonetheless evinces a personal isolation through a narrating voice more vulnerable and idiosyncratically subjective than the 'good daughter' benignity of many of her Warrington poems. What pushes the poem beyond the limits of the urban and rural moralized ruin poem of the eighteenth century, and what makes it as Romantic as it is rationalist, is the way it reiterates Romanticism's appeal to freedom while also acknowledging the defeats of the previous decade. Both the imaginary ruin of London and the imagined empire of Columbus issue from a speaking self who has been unmoored from her previous circles of sociability. There is a poignant identification between Barbauld and the metropolis in the poem; and she is elegiac in her evocation of the fading city whose 'glories pass away' (*SPP* 173, l. 314). In an earlier poem, 'To a Lady, with Some Painted Flowers', Barbauld had made the comparison between female beauty and flowers, which Mary Wollstonecraft criticized in the *Vindication of the Rights of Woman* (1792), calling the comparison 'ignoble'. Barbauld trumps this criticism in *Eighteen Hundred and Eleven* by making the metaphoric link between the metropolis and the flower, 'But fairest flowers expand but to decay' (*SPP* 173, l. 313). Barbauld presents the life of the city on the model of a beautiful woman, who 'knows no second spring' (*SPP* 173, l. 316), and, in so doing, she both dignifies the problem of female aging and also infuses London's ruins with humanity. *Eighteen Hundred and Eleven* might well be Barbauld's revision of her 'Autumnal Thought' of 1795. The sense of loss that permeates the earlier poem is here attached to a more politically astute understanding of the pathways of defeat and regeneration. While the earlier poem could offer only the recompense of the social circle, *Eighteen Hundred and Eleven* compels its speaker into the visionary mode, where she is, as prophetess, utterly isolated but at the same time the medium through which others might see how 'to other climes the Genius soars':

> And pours through feeble souls a higher life,
> Shouts to the mingled tribes from sea to sea
> And swears – Thy world, Columbus, shall be free.
>
> (*SPP* 173, ll. 332–4)

Being old, beyond the claims of a husband and the claims of beauty, Barbauld is able to speak in a voice that approaches that 'citizen' she had invoked in her anonymous 1790 *Address to the Opposers of the Repeal*.

As William Keach has detailed, the reception of *Eighteen Hundred and Eleven* was poisonous. The *Eclectic Review* pronounced, 'The whole tone of it is in a most extraordinary degree unkindly and unpatriotic – we had almost said unfilial.' The Tory *Quarterly Review* attacked her for her unfeminine behaviour: 'We had hoped, indeed, that the empire might have been saved without the intervention of a lady author.' Rather than fading from view as a distinguished pedagogue from a previous century, Barbauld was foregrounded again as a radical, and this gave her an unusually complex public image: prim and stern schoolmarm, and wild-eyed Cassandra. In 1825, the year of Barbauld's death, she was remembered as a Romantic radical, and her fairly anodyne 1795 poem, 'To the Poor', was hauled out as evidence of how 'her patriotic enthusiasm ran away with her understanding and disqualified her judgement'.[23]

BARBAULD AND ROBINSON ON THE SAME LEAF

In 1800 George Nicholson, a publisher near Ludlow, issued a volume of *Odes, by George Dyer, A. L. Barbauld, M. Robinson, J. Ogilvie, etc.*[24] This may be the only contemporary collection to contain poems by both Robinson and Barbauld, including Robinson's 'To Meditation' and Barbauld's 'To Content', 'To Wisdom', and 'To Spring'. The sixty-two-page booklet includes poems by divers hands, including those by poets and radicals Peter Pindar, a close friend of Mary Robinson, and George Dyer, a member of the Aikin set. The chief outlet for *Odes* in London was through H. D. Symonds, Paternoster Row. Henry Symonds had been part of the book trade in radical London and had been arrested and jailed for two years in 1793 for selling Part II of Thomas Paine's *The Rights of Man*. All the poems in the booklet are on themes of retirement and reflection: there are three poems on 'Content' and 'Content-ment', two addressed to 'Wisdom', and ones on 'Reflection', 'Melancholy', 'Meditation', and 'Solitude'. It is a sad booklet, suffused with the voices of resignation and retreat of radicals and reformers and bluestockings and sold by a bookseller recently associated with Paine's red-hot republicanism. But Romantic poetry was founded at the meeting place of En-lightenment theories of liberty and enfranchisement and the poetics of subjectivity and sensibility. London animated the impulses of liberty, and the freedoms it gave women such as Robinson and Barbauld meant that the poetics of subjectivity could be raised from the polite to the passionate. The booklet of *Odes* is not exactly what we would call Romantic poetry, but it sketches out the topics that Romantic and sentimental poets such as Wordsworth and Keats and Landon and Hemans will make their own.

It was, I believe, always the case that Mary Robinson moved with the Zeitgeist, and made herself into a series of living tableaux of the spirit of the age. The end of her life, spent in her cottage in Old Windsor as she finished her sentimental story of herself in the *Memoirs* and readied for publication her volume of *Lyrical Tales*, foreshadows the ethos of respectability that would flourish in the next forty years in middle-class circles. This may be something of a disappointment to those of us who admire her cultural radicalism and her personal refusal of 'meekiness'. But she was most radically a version of the 'Self-Made Man' of the nineteenth century. Socially and economically unstable, but prodigiously talented, she took her chances and made her way – self-reliant, ambitious, and at times, ruthless. Quite differently, Mrs Barbauld's personal history was grounded in a strong and stable family of leading Dissenters, who helped to create and maintain the values of 'practical rationality' in the late eighteenth century. In the radical years, and later when she wrote *Eighteen Hundred and Eleven*, Barbauld's most deeply founded self-confidence and entitlement gave her the privilege of political pronouncement that Robinson might have produced only at the most radical moments of Charles James Fox's ascendance. The two women pass each other as sensibility becomes more rational, and as rationality becomes more passionate. As their bodies failed them through illness and age, the mental powers of the two women can be seen in their strength: Robinson continuing her daily work as writer and editor until the day she died, Barbauld intermittently emerging from her 'good daughter, sister, wife' role to assert her powerful intellect. Robinson's ability to keep producing herself in different forms suggests not that she was without identity but that her identity was so strong as to obviate the need for the appearance of self-congruence. Barbauld's continued assertion of the core values of her world – devotion, reason, kindness, and the belief in the possibility of a global community of speakers, readers, and writers – was met with both embarrassment and hostility from both Whigs and Tories from 1812 until her death in 1825 at the age of 82. Three years later the Corporation and Test acts were repealed, and Dissenters were received fully into the political apparatus, and, with that integration, some of the purity of the Dissenting vision of political life changed into the pragmatic compromises that articulate civil society.

Barbauld's political and intellectual radicalism remained an admirable resource for her and her immediate community of family and friends until her death, many of them her earliest friends and companions at Warrington. Robinson's cultural radicalism meant that the *dramatis personae* of her world were constantly altering, and the overlapping groups she moved in chart a path from the *demi-monde* to the drawing room, as she created the cultural fashions of the coming generations of Romantic and sentimental poetics. In the twenty-first century, Mary Robinson has become our contemporary, a fascinating shape-shifter and chancer, though it may be that Barbauld's values can offer answers to our own pressing political dilemmas.

Notes

CHAPTER 1. SENSE AND SENSIBILITY

1. Isobel Armstrong, 'The Gush of the Feminine: How Can We Read Women's Poetry of the Romantic Period?', in Paula Feldman and Theresa M. Kelley (eds.), *Romantic Women Writers: Voices and Countervoices* (Hanover, NH: University of New England Press, 1995), 13–32.
2. William McCarthy, ' "We Hoped the Woman was Going to Appear": Repression, Desire, and Gender in Anna Laetitia Barbauld's Early Poems', in Feldman and Kelley, *Romantic Women Writers*, 113–37; Eleanor Ty, 'Engendering a Female Subject: Mary Robinson's (Re)Presentations of the Self', *English Studies in Canada*, 21 (1995), 407–33.
3. Quoted in William Keach, 'A Regency Prophecy and the End of Anna Barbauld's Career', *Studies in Romanticism*, 33 (1994), 569. From the *Quarterly Review*, 7 (1812), 309.
4. Laurence Goldstein, *Ruins and Empire: The Evolution of a Theme in Augustan and Romantic Literature* (London: Ferrer and Simons, 1977); Anne Janowitz, *England's Ruins: Poetic Purpose and the National Landscape* (Oxford: Blackwell, 1990), 20–53.
5. Newcombe Cappe, *Discourses on Devotional Subjects, to which are Prefixed Memoirs of his Life, by Catherine Cappe* (London: Johnson, 1805), pp. xiv–xv.
6. Any work on Mary Robinson owes an enormous debt to the scholarship of Judith Pascoe, whose study *Romantic Theatricality: Gender, Poetry, Spectatorship* (Ithaca, NY: Cornell University Press, 1977) argued the case for Robinson's singular achievements and demonstrated how hard won they had been.
7. The best biography of Robinson in the context of her times is Robert D. Bass, *The Green Dragoon: The Lives of Banastre Tarleton and Mary Robinson* (London: Alvin Redman, 1957).

8. Ty, 'Engendering a Female Subject'.

CHAPTER 2. POETIC VOCATION AND POLITE LETTERS: THE 1760s AND 1770s

1. H. McLachlan, *Warrington Academy: Its History and Influence* (Manchester: Chetham Society, 1943), 23.
2. Joseph Priestley, *Memoirs* (Bath: Adams & Dart, 1970), 88.
3. William Enfield, *A Funeral Sermon, Occasioned by the Death of the Late Rev. John Aikin, D.D.* (Warrington: W. Eyres, for J. Johnson, London, 1781), 18.
4. Francis E. Mineka, *The Dissidence of Dissent:* The Monthly Repository, *1806–1825* (Chapel Hill, NC: University of North Carolina Press, 1944), 39, 44. For the importance of the *Monthly Repository* to Victorian poetry, see Isobel Armstrong, *Victorian Poetry: Poetry, Poetics, and Politics* (London: Routledge, 1993), 25 ff.
5. The phrase was used by William Turner to describe the pedagogic style of John Aikin DD, in Turner's 'Historical Account of the Warrington Academy', *Monthly Repository*, 8 (1813), 169.
6. Lucy Aikin, *Memoir of John Aikin, M.D.*, 2 vols. (London: Baldwin, Craddock, & Joy, 1823), and *The Works of Anna Laetitia Barbauld, with a Memoir*, 2 vols. (London: Longman, 1825); Anna Le Breton, *Memoir of Mrs Barbauld, Including Letters and Notices of her Family and Friends* (London: G. Bell, 1874).
7. Betsy Rodgers, *Georgian Chronicle: Mrs Barbauld and her Family* (London: Methuen, 1958).
8. Gilbert Wakefield, *Memoirs* (London: Hodson, 1792), 215; Aikin quoted in Anna Le Breton, *Memoir of Mrs Barbauld*, 35; for a different reading of the meaning of Barbauld's interest in the domestic, see Josephine McDonagh, 'Barbauld's Domestic Economy', in Anne Janowitz (ed.), *Romanticism and Gender* (Leicester: English Association, 1998), 62–77.
9. Lucy Aikin, *John Aikin*, i. 10.
10. Michael R. Watts, *The Dissenters*, 2 vols. (Oxford: Clarendon Press, 1978), i. 366.
11. Rodgers, *Georgian Chronicle*, 50; Henry A. Bright, *A Historical Sketch of Warrington Academy* (Liverpool: Brakell, 1859).
12. Lucy Aikin, *Anna Laetitia Barbauld*, i, p. vi.
13. Ibid., p. vii.
14. Anna Le Breton, *Memoir of Mrs Barbauld*, 47.
15. Priestley, *Memoirs*, 89.
16. McLachlan, *Warrington Academy*, 82.

17. Paul Langford, *A Polite and Commercial People: England 1727–1783* (Oxford: Oxford University Press, 1992), 59–122.
18. Anna Le Breton, *Memoir of Mrs Barbauld*, 38.
19. Bright, *Historical Sketch*, 12.
20. Lucy Aikin, *Anna Laetitia Barbauld*, i, p. xiii.
21. Lucy Aikin, *John Aikin*, i. 19.
22. Samuel Rogers, *Table-Talk*, ed. Revd. Alexander Dyce (London: Rogers, 1887), 82.
23. William Woodfall, *Monthly Review*, 48 (1773), 54–9, 133–7.
24. John Guillory, 'The English Common Place: Lineages of the Topographical Genre', *Critical Quarterly*, 33 (1991), 8.
25. David Garrick, *Annual Register*, 18 (1775), cited in Rodgers, *Georgian Chronicle*, 61.
26. For two very different and impressive readings of *Eighteen Hundred and Eleven*, see William Keach, 'A Regency Prophecy and the End of Anna Barbauld's Career', *Studies in Romanticism*, 33 (1994), 569–77, and Lucy Newlyn, *The Anxiety of Reception: Romanticism and the Rise of the Reader* (Oxford: Oxford University Press), 136–69.
27. Bright, *Historical Sketch*, 22, 28.
28. Woodfall, *Monthly Review*, 133.
29. Samuel Taylor Coleridge, *Table Talk*, ed. Carl Woodring, 2 vols. (Princeton: Princeton University Press, 1990), i. 564–5; Bright, *Historical Sketch*, 21.
30. Lucy Aikin, *John Aikin*, ii. 297.
31. Elizabeth Eger, on the other hand, finds Barbauld to be 'an outsider in a community of outsiders' at Warrington; see Elizabeth Eger, 'The Nine Living Muses of Great Britain (1779): Women, Reason, and Literary Community in Eighteenth-Century Britain', dissertation (Cambridge, 1999), 214; William McCarthy, ' "We Hoped the Woman was Going to Appear": Repression, Desire, and Gender in Anna Laetitia Barbauld's Early Poems', in Paula Feldman and Theresa M. Kelley (eds.), *Romantic Women Writers: Voices and Countervoices* (Hanover, NH: University of New England Press, 1995), 113–37.
32. W. Jackson Bate, *The Burden of the Past and the English Poet* (London: Harvard University Press, 1970), 38.
33. *Horace Walpole's Correspondence*, ed. W. S. Lewis (New Haven: Yale University Press, 1937–), xv. 331.
34. Ibid. ix. 90, 255.
35. Laetitia Matilda Hawkins, *Memoirs, Anecdotes, Facts, and Opinions*, 2 vols. (London: Longman, 1824), ii. 27.
36. James Boaden, *Memoirs of the Life of John Philip Kemble*, 2 vols. (London: Longman, 1825), ii. 136.

37. See Jerome McGann on Schiller in his *Poetics of Sensibility: A Revolution in Literary Style* (Oxford: Oxford University Press, 1996), 119–26.

CHAPTER 3. ACTRESS AND PEDAGOGUE: 1774–1789

1. Henry A. Bright, *A Historical Sketch of Warrington Academy* (Liverpool: Brakell, 1859), 22, 28.
2. H. McLachlan, *Warrington Academy: Its History and Influence* (Manchester: Chetham Society, 1943), 87.
3. *Notes and Queries*, NS 11 (1922), 53.
4. John Towill Rutt, *Life and Correspondence of Joseph Priestley*, 2 vols. (London: Hunter, 1831), i. 284.
5. William McCarthy, 'The Celebrated Academy at Palgrave: A Documentary History of Anna Letitia Barbauld's School', *The Age of Johnson*, 8 (1997), 282.
6. Grace A. Ellis, *Memoir, Letters, and a Selection from the Poems and Prose Writings of Anna Laetitia* Barbauld, 2 vols. (Boston: J. R. Osgood, 1874, 1880), i. 100.
7. McCarthy, 'Celebrated Academy', app. III.
8. Ibid. 288.
9. Philip Hemery Le Breton, *Memoirs, Miscellanies and Letters of the Late Lucy Aikin* (London: Longman, 1864), 274.
10. Cited in Betsy Rodgers, *Georgian Chronicle: Mrs Barbauld and her Family* (London: Methuen, 1958), 76.
11. William Turner, 'Mrs Barbauld', *Newcastle Magazine*, 4 (1825), 230.
12. McCarthy, 'Celebrated Academy', 307.
13. Harriet Martineau, *Autobiography*, ed. W. M. Chapman, 3 vols. (London, 1877), i. 34.
14. Gerald P. Tyson, *Joseph Johnson: A Liberal Publisher* (Iowa City: University of Iowa Press, 1979), 84; William Beloe, *The Sexagenarian; or the Recollections of a Literary Life*, 2 vols. (London: Rivington, 1817), i. 345.
15. Ellis, *Memoir*, i. 117.
16. Ibid. 100.
17. Elizabeth Eger, 'Representing Culture: "The Nine Living Muses of Great Britain" (1779)', in Elizabeth Eger, Charlotte Grant, et al. (eds.), *Women, Writing and the Public Sphere 1700–1830* (Cambridge: Cambridge University Press, 2001), 104–26.
18. Cited in Rodgers, *Georgian Chronicle*, 71.
19. Anon., *The Memoirs of Perdita* (London: Glister, 1784).
20. *Horace Walpole's Correspondence*, ed. W. S. Lewis (New Haven: Yale University Press, 1937–), xxxv. 523.

21. Ellis, *Memoir*, i. 117.
22. For a survey of the portraits, see John Ingamells, *Mrs Robinson and her Portraits* (London: Wallace Collection, 1978).
23. Eleanor Ty, 'Engendering a Female Subject: Mary Robinson's (Re)Presentations of the Self', *English Studies in Canada*, 21 (1995), 412.
24. Laetitia Matilda Hawkins, *Memoirs, Anecdotes, Facts, and Opinions*, 2 vols. (London: Longman, 1824), i. 24.
25. Robert D. Bass, *The Green Dragoon: The Lives of Banastre Tarleton and Mary Robinson* (London: Alvin Redman, 1957), 219.
26. Ibid. 225.
27. Hawkins, *Memoirs*, i. 34.
28. Anthony Pasquin, *The New Brighton Guide*, 6th edn. (London: Symonds, 1796), 3.
29. Bass, *Green Dragoon*, 252.
30. Hawkins, *Memoirs*, i. 35.
31. Judith Pascoe, *Romantic Theatricality: Gender, Poetry, Spectatorship* (Ithaca, NY: Cornell University Press, 1977), 69.
32. James Boaden, *Memoirs of the Life of John Philip Kemble*, 2 vols. (London: Longman, 1825), i. 137.

CHAPTER 4. RADICAL LONDON: 1789–1791

1. L. G. Mitchell, *Charles James Fox* (Oxford: Oxford University Press, 1992), 111, 241–50.
2. *Morning Post*, 19 July 1791, cited in ibid. 119.
3. Gerald P. Tyson, *Joseph Johnson: A Liberal Publisher* (Iowa City: University of Iowa Press, 1979), 56.
4. Lucy Aikin, *The Works of Anna Laetitia Barbauld, with a Memoir*, 2 vols. (London: Longman, 1825), i, pp. xxxii–xxxiii.
5. Tyson, *Joseph Johnson*, 67–8, 43–4.
6. Leslie F. Chard, 'Joseph Johnson: Father of the Book Trade', *Bulletin of the New York Public Library*, 79 (1975), 63.
7. Tyson, *Joseph Johnson*, 93.
8. William Keate, *A Free Examination of Dr. Price's and Dr. Priestley's Sermons, with a post-script containing some strictures upon 'An Address to the Opposers of the Repeal of the Corporation and Test Acts'* (London: Dodsley, 1790), 55–64.
9. Ibid. 55, 64.
10. Henry A. Bright, *A Historical Sketch of Warrington Academy* (Liverpool: Brakell, 1859), 22.
11. *Horace Walpole's Correspondence*, ed. W. S. Lewis (New Haven: Yale University Press, 1937–), xi. 169, 320.

12. Betsy Rodgers, *Georgian Chronicle: Mrs Barbauld and her Family* (London: Methuen, 1958), 115.
13. Jon Mee, ' "Reciprocal expressions of kindness": Robert Merry, Della Cruscanism and the Limits of Sociability', in Gillian Russell and Clara Tuite (eds.), *Romantic Sociability: Social Networks and Literary Culture in Britain 1770–1840* (Cambridge: Cambridge University Press, 2002), 113.
14. 'Counter-Remonstrance', in John Aikin, *Poems* (London: Johnson, 1791), p. v.
15. Ellis, *Memoir*, i. 198.
16. Gilbert Wakefield, *Memoirs* (London: Hodson, 1792), 204.
17. Ibid. 211.
18. Ibid. 2.
19. William Keach, 'Barbauld, Romanticism, and the Survival of Dissent', in Anne Janowitz (ed.), *Romanticism and Gender* (Leicester: English Association, 1998), 56.
20. Rodgers, *Georgian Chronicle*, 189; Anna Le Breton, *Memoir of Mrs Barbauld, Including Letters and Notices of her Family and Friends* (London: G. Bell, 1874), 81.
21. William Godwin, *Enquiry concerning Political Justice, etc.*, ed. F. E. L. Priestley, 3 vols. (Toronto: University of Toronto Press, 1946), iii. 146.
22. *Public Characters of 1800–1801* (London: Richard Phillips, 1807), 336.
23. Stanley Morison, *John Bell, 1745–1831* (Private Publication at Cambridge University, 1930), 43, 14, 8, 10, 41.
24. Markman Ellis, *Politics of Sensibility: Race, Gender and Commerce in the Sentimental Novel* (Cambridge: Cambridge University Press, 1996).
25. Judith Pascoe, *Romantic Theatricality: Gender, Poetry, Spectatorship* (Ithaca, NY: Cornell University Press, 1977), 25.
26. Ibid. 151.
27. Mitchell, *Fox*, 111.

CHAPTER 5. BARBAULD AND ROBINSON AMONGST THE ROMANTICS

1. Stuart Curran, 'Mary Robinson's *Lyrical Tales* in Context', in Carol Shiner Wilson and Joel Haefner (eds.), *Re-Visioning Romanticism: British Women Writers, 1776–1837* (Philadelphia: University of Pennsylvania Press, 1994), 21.
2. 'A Description of London', in A. N. Wilson (ed.), *The Faber Book of London* (London: Faber, 1993), p. vi.

3. James Boaden, *Memoirs of the Life of John Philip Kemble*, 2 vols. (London: Longman, 1825), ii. 136–7.

4. Curran, *'Lyrical Tales* in Context', 19.

5. Kenneth Curry, *The Contributions of Robert Southey to the* Morning Post (Tuscaloosa, Ala.: University of Alabama Press, 1984), 1.

6. For a detailed and controversial assessment of Coleridge's borrowings, see Norman Fruman, *Coleridge, the Damaged Archangel* (London: George Allen & Unwin, 1971), *passim*.

7. Martin J. Levy, 'Coleridge, Mary Robinson, and *Kubla Khan*', *Charles Lamb Bulletin*, NS 77 (1992), 159.

8. Samuel Taylor Coleridge, *Collected Letters*, ed. Earl Leslie Griggs 6 vols. (Oxford: Clarendon Press, 1966–71), i. 562.

9. *The Letters of Dorothy and William Wordsworth*, ed. Ernest de Selincourt, 6 vols., *The Early Years, 1787–1805*, rev. Chester L. Shaver (Oxford: Clarendon Press, 1967), i. 297.

10. Joseph Cottle, *Early Recollections, Chiefly Relating to the Late Samuel Taylor Coleridge*, 2 vols. (London: Longman, 1837), ii. 24.

11. Curran, *'Lyrical Tales in Context'*, 29.

12. Betsy Rodgers, *Georgian Chronicle: Mrs Barbauld and her Family* (London: Methuen, 1958), 129–30.

13. Tyson, *Johnson*, 163; see also Jane Worthington Smyser, 'The Trial and Imprisonment of Joseph Johnson, Bookseller', *Bulletin of the New York Public Library*, 77 (1974), 418–35, and Leslie F. Chard, 'Joseph Johnson: Father of the Book Trade', *Bulletin of the New York Public Library*, 79 (1975), 51–82.

14. John Aikin, 'To Gilbert Wakefield, A.B. on his Liberation from Prison', *Monthly Magazine* (June 1801), 422; Gilbert Wakefield, 'To John Aikin, M.D.', *Monthly Magazine* (July 1801), 513; see also Lucy Aikin, 'To the Memory of Gilbert Wakefield', *Monthly Magazine* (Oct. 1801), 220–1.

15. Lucy Aikin, *John Aikin*, i. 247.

16. Coleridge, *Collected Letters*, i. 137.

17. Samuel Taylor Coleridge, *Table Talk*, ed. Carl Woodring, 2 vols. (Princeton: Princeton University Press, 1990), i. 564–5.

18. Mary Jacobus, *Tradition and Experiment in Wordsworth's* Lyrical Ballads, 1798 (Oxford: Clarendon Press, 1976), 209.

19. *Monthly Magazine* (Jan. 1796), 118.

20. J. W. Robberds, *Memoir of the Life and Writings of William Taylor*, 2 vols. (London: Murray, 1843), i. 92.

21. Rodgers, *Georgian Chronicle*, 136, 139.

22. Anne Mellor, 'The Female Poet and the Poetess: Two Traditions of British Women's Poetry, 1780–1830', *Studies in Romanticism*, 36 (1997), 271; Lucy Newlyn, *The Anxiety of Reception: Romanticism*

and the Rise of the Reader (Oxford: Oxford University Press); William Keach, 'A Regency Prophecy and the End of Anna Barbauld's Career', *Studies in Romanticism*, 33 (1994), 569–77.

23. *Literary Gazette*, 24 Sept. 1825, 611.
24. George Dyer, A. L. Barbauld, M. Robinson, J. Ogilvie, etc., *Odes* (Ludlow: G. Nicolson, 1800).

Select Bibliography

MARY ROBINSON

Early Editions

Poems (London: C. Parker, 1775).
Captivity, a Poem and Celadon, A Tale (London: T. Beckett, 1777).
Ainsi va le monde (London: J. Bell, 1790).
Poems (London: J. Bell, 1791).
Poems, 2 vols. (London: J. Evans and T. Beckett, 1793).
Sappho and Phaon, in a series of Legitimate Sonnets (London: Hookham, 1796).
Letter to the Women of England, on the Injustice of Mental Subordination (London: Longman, 1799).
The False Friend: A Domestic Story, 4 vols. (London: T. N. Longman and O. Rees, 1799).
The Natural Daughter: A Novel, 2 vols. (London: T. N. Longman and O. Rees, 1799).
Lyrical Tales (London and Bristol: T. N. Longman and O. Rees/Biggs & Co., 1800).
Poetical Works of the Late Mrs. Mary Robinson, 3 vols. (London: R. Phillips, 1806).

Modern Editions

Perdita: The Memoirs of Mary Robinson, ed. M. J. Levy (London: Peter Owen, 1994).
Mary Robinson: Selected Poems, ed. Judith Pascoe (Ontario: Broadview Press, 2000).

115

ANNA BARBAULD

Early Editions

Poems (London: J. Johnson, 1773). Further editions in 1773, 1774, 1776–7.

Hymns in Prose for Children (London: J. Johnson, 1781).

An Address to the Opposers of the Repeal of the Corporation and Test Acts, 2nd edn. (London: J. Johnson, 1790).

Civic Sermons to the People (London: J. Johnson, 1792).

Epistle to William Wilberforce, Esq. on the Rejection of the Bill for Abolishing the Slave Trade (London: J. Johnson, 1791).

Remarks on Mr. Gilbert Wakefield's Enquiry into the Expediency and Propriety of Public or Social Worship, 2nd edn. (London: Johnson, 1792).

Eighteen Hundred and Eleven (London: J. Johnson, 1812).

Works of Anna Laetitia Barbauld. With a Memoir by Lucy Aikin, 2 vols. (London: Longman, 1825).

Modern Editions

The Poems of Anna Laetitia Barbauld, ed. William McCarthy and Elizabeth Kraft (London: University of Georgia Press, 1994).

Selected Poetry and Prose, ed. William McCarthy and Elizabeth Kraft (Ontario: Broadview Press, 2002).

BIOGRAPHY, HISTORY, AND MEMOIRS

Aikin, Lucy, *Memoir of John Aikin, M.D.*, 2 vols. (London: Baldwin, Craddock, & Joy, 1823).

—— *The Works of Anna Laetitia Barbauld, with a Memoir*, 2 vols. (London: Longman, 1825).

Barrell, John, *Imagining the King's Death: Figurative Treason, Fantasies of Regicide, 1793–1796* (Oxford: Oxford University Press, 2000).

Bass, Robert D., *The Green Dragoon: The Lives of Banastre Tarleton and Mary Robinson* (London: Alvin Redman, 1957).

Beloe, William, *The Sexagenarian; or the Recollections of a Literary Life*, 2 vols. (London: Rivington, 1817).

Boaden, James, *Memoirs of the Life of John Philip Kemble*, 2 vols. (London: Longman, 1825).

Cappe, Newcombe, *Discourses on Devotional Subjects, to which are Prefixed Memoirs of his Life, by Catherine Cappe* (London: Johnson, 1805).

Coleridge, Samuel Taylor, *Table Talk*, ed. Carl Woodring, 2 vols. (Princeton: Princeton University Press, 1990).

Ellis, Grace, *Memoir, Letters, and a Selection from the Poems and Prose Writings of Anna Laetitia Barbauld*, 2 vols. (Boston: J. R. Osgood & Co., 1874, 1880).

Enfield, William, *A Funeral Sermon, Occasioned by the Death of the Late Rev. John Aikin, D.D.* (Warrington: W. Eyres, for J. Johnson, London, 1781).

Ferguson, Moira, *Subject to Others: British Women Writers and Colonial Slavery, 1670–1834* (London: Routledge, 1992).

Goodwin, Albert, *The Friends of Liberty: The English Democratic Movement in the Age of the French Revolution* (Cambridge, MA: Harvard University Press, 1979).

Hawkins, Laetitia Matilda, *Memoirs, Anecdotes, Facts, and Opinions*, 2 vols. (London: Longman, 1824).

Ingamells, John, *Mrs. Robinson and her Portraits* (London: Wallace Collection, 1978).

Langford, Paul, *A Polite and Commercial People: England 1727–1783* (Oxford: Oxford University Press, 1992).

Le Breton, Anna, *Memoir of Mrs Barbauld, Including Letters and Notices of her Family and Friends* (London: G. Bell, 1874).

McCalman, Iain, *Radical Underworld: Prophets, Revolutionaries and Pornographers in London, 1795–1840* (Cambridge: Cambridge University Press, 1988).

McCarthy, William, 'The Celebrated Academy at Palgrave: A Documentary History of Anna Letitia Barbauld's School', *The Age of Johnson*, 8 (1997), 279–392.

McLachlan, H., *Warrington Academy: Its History and Influence* (Manchester: Chetham Society, 1943).

Mineka, Francis E., *The Dissidence of Dissent:* The Monthly Repository, *1806–1825* (Chapel Hill, NC: University of North Carolina Press, 1944).

Mitchell, L. G., *Charles James Fox* (Oxford: Oxford University Press, 1992).

Priestley, Joseph, *Memoirs* (Bath: Adams & Dart, 1970).

Rodgers, Betsy, *Georgian Chronicle: Mrs Barbauld and her Family* (London: Methuen, 1958).

Rogers, Samuel, *Table-Talk*, ed. Revd. Alexander Dyce (London: Rogers, 1887).

Rutt, John Towill, *Life and Correspondence of Joseph Priestley*, 2 vols. (London: Hunter, 1831).

Tyson, Gerald P., *Joseph Johnson: A Liberal Publisher* (Iowa City: University of Iowa Press, 1979).

117

Wakefield, Gilbert, *Memoirs* (London: Hodson, 1792).
Watts, Michael R., *The Dissenters* (Oxford: Clarendon Press, 1978).

CRITICISM

Armstrong, Isobel, 'The Gush of the Feminine: How Can We Read Women's Poetry of the Romantic Period?', in Paula Feldman and Theresa M. Kelley (eds.), *Romantic Women Writers: Voices and Countervoices* (Hanover, NH: University of New England Press, 1995), 13–32.

Barker-Benfield, G. J., *The Culture of Sensibility: Sex and Society in Eighteenth Century Britain* (Chicago: University of Chicago Press, 1992).

Bate, W. Jackson, *The Burden of the Past and the English Poet* (London: Harvard University Press, 1970).

Bright, Henry A., *A Historical Sketch of Warrington* (Liverpool: Brakell, 1859).

Curran, Stuart, 'The "I" Altered', in Anne K. Mellor (ed.), *Romanticism and Feminism* (Bloomington, IN: Indiana University Press, 1988), 185–207.

—— 'Mary Robinson's *Lyrical Tales* in Context', in Carol Shiner Wilson and Joel Haefner (eds.), *Re-Visioning Romanticism: British Women Writers, 1776–1837* (Philadelphia: University of Pennsylvania Press, 1994), 17–35.

Eger, Elizabeth, 'Representing Culture: "The Nine Living Muses of Great Britain" (1779)', in Elizabeth Eger, Charlotte Grant, et al. (eds.), *Women, Writing and the Public Sphere 1700–1830* (Cambridge: Cambridge University Press, 2001), 104–26.

Ellis, Markman, *Politics of Sensibility: Race, Gender and Commerce in the Sentimental Novel* (Cambridge: Cambridge University Press, 1996).

Guillory, John, 'The English Common Place: Lineages of the Topographical Genre', *Critical Quarterly*, 33 (1991), 3–27.

Janowitz, Anne, 'Amiable and Radical Sociability: Anna Barbauld's "Free Familiar Conversation"', in Gillian Russell and Clara Tuite (eds.), *Romantic Sociability: Social Networks and Literary Culture in Britain, 1770–1840* (Cambridge: Cambridge University Press, 2002), 62–81.

Keach, William, 'A Regency Prophecy and the End of Anna Barbauld's Career', *Studies in Romanticism*, 33 (1994), 569–77.

—— 'Barbauld, Romanticism, and the Survival of Dissent', in Anne Janowitz (ed.), *Romanticism and Gender* (Leicester: English Association, 1998), 44–61.

Levy, Martin J., 'Coleridge, Mary Robinson, and *Kubla Khan*', *Charles Lamb Bulletin*, NS 77 (1992), 156–66.

McCarthy, William, ' "We Hoped the Woman was Going to Appear": Repression, Desire, and Gender in Anna Laetitia Barbauld's Early Poems', in Paula Feldman and Theresa M. Kelley (eds.), *Romantic Women Writers: Voices and Countervoices* (Hanover, NH: University of New England Press, 1995), 113–37.

McDonagh, Josephine, 'Barbauld's Domestic Economy', in Anne Janowitz (ed.), *Romanticism and Gender* (Leicester: English Association, 1998), 62–77.

McGann, Jerome, *Poetics of Sensibility: A Revolution in Literary Style* (Oxford: Oxford University Press, 1996).

Mellor, Anne, 'The Female Poet and the Poetess: Two Traditions of British Women's Poetry, 1780–1830', *Studies in Romanticism*, 36 (1997), 261–76.

Newlyn, Lucy, *Reading, Writing, and Romanticism: The Anxiety of Reception* (Oxford: Oxford University Press, 2000).

Mee, Jon, ' "Reciprocal Expressions of Kindness": Robert Merry, Della Cruscanism, and the Limits of Sociability', in Gillian Russell and Clara Tuite (eds.), *Romantic Sociability: Social Networks and Literary Culture in Britain, 1770–1840* (Cambridge: Cambridge University Press, 2002), 104–22.

Pascoe, Judith, *Romantic Theatricality: Gender, Poetry, Spectatorship* (Ithaca, NY: Cornell University Press, 1977).

Ross, Marlon, 'Configurations of Female Reform: The Woman Writer and the Tradition of Dissent', in Carol Shiner Wilson and Joel Haefner (ed.), *Re-Visioning Romanticism: British Women Writers, 1776–1837* (Philadelphia: University of Pennsylvania Press, 1994), 91–110.

Ty, Eleanor, 'Engendering a Female Subject: Mary Robinson's (Re)Presentations of the Self', *English Studies in Canada*, 21 (1995), 407–33.

Index

Recent and Forthcoming Titles in the New Series of

WRITERS AND THEIR WORK

WRITERS AND THEIR WORK

RECENT & FORTHCOMING TITLES

RECENT & FORTHCOMING TITLES

TITLES IN PREPARATION

Title	Author
Title	Author
Fleur Adcock	*Janet Wilson*
Ama Ata Aidoo	*Nana Wilson-Tagoe*
Matthew Arnold	*Kate Campbell*
Margaret Atwood	*Marion Wynne-Davies*
John Banville	*Peter Dempsey*
William Barnes	*Christopher Ricks*
Black British Writers	*Deidre Osborne*
William Blake	*Steven Vine*
Charlotte Brontë	*Stevie Davies*
Robert Browning	*John Woodford*
Basil Bunting	*Martin Stannard*
John Bunyan	*Tamsin Spargoe*
Coriolanus	*Anita Pacheco*
Cymbeline	*Peter Swaab*
Douglas Dunn	*David Kennedy*
David Edgar	*Peter Boxall*
T. S. Eliot	*Colin MacCabe*
J. G. Farrell	*John McLeod*
Nadine Gordimer	*Lewis Nkosi*
Geoffrey Grigson	*R. M. Healey*
David Hare	*Jeremy Ridgman*
Ted Hughes	*Susan Bassnett*
The Imagist Poets	*Andrew Thacker*
Ben Jonson	*Anthony Johnson*
A. L. Kennedy	*Dorothy McMillan*
Jack Kerouac	*Michael Hrebebiak*
Jamaica Kincaid	*Susheila Nasta*
Rudyard Kipling	*Jan Montefiore*
Rosamond Lehmann	*Judy Simon*
Una Marson & Louise Bennett	*Alison Donnell*
Norman MacCaig	*Alasdair Macrae*
Thomas Middleton	*Hutchings & Bromham*
John Milton	*Nigel Smith*
Much Ado About Nothing	*John Wilders*
R. K. Narayan	*Shirley Chew*
New Woman Writers	*Marion Shaw/Lyssa Randolph*
Ngugi wa Thiong'o	*Brendon Nicholls*
Religious Poets of the 17th Century	*Helen Wilcox*
Revenge Tragedy	*Janet Clare*
Samuel Richardson	*David Deeming*
Olive Schreiner	*Carolyn Burdett*
Sam Selvon	*Ramchand & Salick*
Olive Senior	*Denise de Canes Narain*
Mary Shelley	*Catherine Sharrock*
Charlotte Smith & Helen Williams	*Angela Keane*
Ian Crichton Smith	*Colin Nicholson*
R. L. Stevenson	*David Robb*
Tom Stoppard	*Nicholas Cadden*
Elizabeth Taylor	*N. R. Reeve*
Dylan Thomas	*Chris Wiggington*
Three Avant-Garde Poets	*Peter Middleton*
Three Lyric Poets	*William Rowe*
Derek Walcott	*Stephen Regan*

TITLES IN PREPARATION

Title	Author
Jeanette Winterson	*Gina Vitello*
Women's Poetry at the Fin de Siècle	*Anna Vadillo*
William Wordsworth	*Nicola Trott*